PENGUIN BOOKS
AUDREY EYTON'S F-PLUS

As well as being the author of Britain's bestselling diet of all time, *The F-Plan Diet*, Audrey Eyton is the woman who can justly claim to have invented that now popular feature of every magazine stall – the slimming magazine. When she and her partner founded *Slimming Magazine* seventeen years ago it was the first publication in the world to specialize in the subject. The publication was an instant success and has continued to be the dominating bestseller despite the many rival magazines which have followed.

For many years Audrey Eyton edited *Slimming Magazine* herself, and later became Editorial Director. During their years of ownership (the company was sold in 1980) she and her partner also started Ragdale Hall Health Farm and founded and developed one of Britain's largest chains of slimming clubs. Mrs Eyton continues to work as a consultant to the company.

During her many years of specialization in the problems of weight control and healthy eating, Mrs Eyton has worked with most of the world's leading nutritional, medical and psychological experts. No writer has a greater knowledge and understanding of the subject. She has a nineteen-year-old son and lives in Kensington and Kent.

AUDREY EYTON'S

F-PLUS

Recipes and menus created and written by

Joyce M. Hughes

PENGUIN BOOKS

Penguin Books Ltd, Harmondsworth, Middlesex, England
Viking Penguin Inc., 40 West 23rd Street, New York, New York 10010, U.S.A.
Penguin Books Australia Ltd, Ringwood, Victoria, Australia
Penguin Books Canada Ltd, 2801 John Street, Markham, Ontario, Canada L3R 1B4
Penguin Books (N.Z.) Ltd, 182–190 Wairau Road, Auckland 10, New Zealand

First published as *Audrey Eyton's Even Easier F-Plan* by Allen Lane 1984
Published in Penguin Books as *Audrey Eyton's F-Plus* 1985
Reprinted 1985, 1987

Introduction copyright © Audrey Eyton, 1984
Menus, recipes and interlinking text copyright © Joyce Hughes, 1984
All rights reserved

Made and printed in Great Britain by
Richard Clay Ltd, Bungay, Suffolk
Set in Monophoto Photina

CONTENTS

CONTENTS

ACKNOWLEDGEMENTS

Our thanks to Sue Horsman who typed the manuscript quickly and superbly, frequently correcting errors unprompted, and to home economist Sandra Tomsett, who devised and tested many of the recipes in the 'Keen Cook's' and 'Freezer-owner's' F-Plan menus.

YES, EVEN EASIER F-PLAN!

You have already heard, or discovered for yourself, that the F-Plan is the easiest slimming method ever devised. Now you can be *spoon-fed* with your daily dose of health-protecting, weight-loss-assisting dietary fibre.

How much dietary fibre should you consume in a day? Don't worry. Just follow any of the dozens of ready-planned complete day's menus in this book and you will get the right quantity of fibre from the correct varied sources. How do you count the calories? Don't count – again, just follow the menus; the calories are ready counted for controlled weight loss.

The first F-Plan book, which made publishing history when it was released two years ago, offered a wide range of high-fibre, low-calorie meals from which you could put together your own high-fibre slimming menus. The second, *The F-Plan Calorie and Fibre Chart*, added further eat-your-own-thing flexibility. Now this third companion volume adds a new element of effortlessness. No need to add up or work out what you are going to eat. Just flick through, pick out the kinds of menu which suit you best, and follow one each day.

Hate to cook? Haven't time to fuss? On pp. 156–78 you'll find a wide range of F-Plan daily menus making maximum use of canned and packaged food. Rushing off to work and wondering how to get an F-Plan diet lunch? The ready-planned F-Plan menus with packed lunches starting on p. 61 will be just right for you. Prefer to plan ahead and cook most of your F-Plan meals in advance? Sensible you. On p. 246 you'll see how to do it, making maximum use of your freezer.

Whether man, woman or child you will find ready-planned F-Plan full-day menus to suit you and your life-style in this book. We've done all the thinking and planning and putting-it-together for you so that all you need to do to get slim and fit is to make it (or buy it) and eat it. That's what we mean by 'even easier F-Plan'. Over to you.

INTRODUCTION

Except for those who have recently returned from a two-year expedition into the South American interior (in which case, living off the land, they have probably inadvertently been following it already!) the F-Plan diet needs little further introduction to the British public. In two years the name has become familiar to us all. To compare its all-time record-breaking sale in Britain, now in the region of two million, with that of any diet in the past would be similar to comparing the size of a baked potato with that of a baked bean.

Travel to the furthest ends of the earth and *The F-Plan* provides an instant topic of communication. Breathe its name, if you will, next time you visit Reykjavik and you will discover that there is an Icelandic edition. Travel to New Zealand and you will learn how it made history there – the fastest-selling book of all (fiction or non-fiction) in the publishing records of the country. In Australia it broke all diet-book sales records, in Canada it shot to the top of the bestseller lists within days of arrival. In America, birthplace of all the previous diet-book blockbusters, it overcame initial scepticism – 'A diet from *Britain*?' – by becoming the first imported diet to hit the bestseller lists month after month. Even Islam has embraced it with an alcohol-free edition. It has become the best-selling diet in the world.

Now why on earth, literally, has the F-Plan caused such a fuss?

It is, understandably, in the nature of the overweight person to seek eagerly for the revolutionary new method which will provide an easier solution to that stubborn weight problem. It is in the nature of the diet-book writer to try to provide it. However, the diet-book writer of yesteryear laboured under the difficulty of having to *invent* a 'revolution' – a task which the fearless and imaginative did not hesitate to tackle. As one leading nutritionist remarked, plaintively, of a famous American best-selling diet of a few years ago: 'I have no objection at all to it being top of the bestseller list. But why did they list it in the non-fiction rather than the fiction section?'

However, quietly, in the universities and research laboratories of the affluent world, a remarkable thing has been emerging over the past few years. A nutritional revolution, a *REAL* one. A major and almost complete about-turn in the beliefs about which foods we should eat more abundantly and which we should ration more stringently if we are concerned about becoming slim and protecting our health.

To put it very simplistically, animal foods were in the recent past considered the outstanding source of most goodness and animal protein acquired an almost magical aura of virtue. Lucky us, in the affluent world, to be able to indulge lavishly in meat and cream while the rest of the world had to struggle along on — well, peasant food like beans, root vegetables and coarse-ground breads.

When struggling to reduce our weight, which somehow continued to increase on this regime, we were urged to keep eating all that really valuable animal food and cut out the second-class foods that really didn't matter much: potatoes, bread, cereal foods and things of that ilk.

There was a snag. On our high-animal-food diets, we in the affluent world were getting fatter and fatter. We were also being killed off at an alarming rate by coronaries and illnesses like cancer of the colon which were hardly known in countries existing on a much higher proportion of cereal, fruit and vegetable food. What we were eating, over-abundantly, as an unavoidable part of our high-animal-food diet, was a large quantity of fat — and recent research has discovered close links between this high fat intake and both obesity and coronary heart disease. All animal foods, even the leaner meats, contain a significant amount of fat.

What we weren't eating was a seemingly unimportant substance found in those peasant foods like beans and unrefined cereals — dietary fibre. Again, recent nutritional research has indicated that the importance of this substance has been vastly underestimated both in helping us to control our weight and protect our health against the major Western killer diseases.

Pity the poor dieter. Prior to the nutritional about-turn, he was being urged to eat many of the most fattening foods (hard cheese at 120 calories an ounce, for instance!) and to cut out the most helpful foods like root vegetables, cereals and bread, which could fill him up with a much lower intake of calories.

Pity the poor health enthusiast. In chewing his way through quantities of steak and swooshing down gallons of full-cream milk he appears to have been clogging up his arteries with coronary-inducing cholesterol.

It was no one's fault, really. Nutrition is a relatively new and inexact science in the early stages of discovery and the leaders of the profession are now willing and anxious to say, albeit in their own language: 'Look chaps, we got it wrong.' They do so, for instance, in the 1983 Health Education Council publication, *A Discussion Paper on Proposals for Nutritional Guidelines for Health Education in Britain* (nutritionists were never strong on fun titles!), with this statement:

The previous nutritional advice in the UK to limit the intake of all carbohydrates as a means of weight control now runs counter to current thinking and contrary to the present proposals for a nutrition policy for the population as a whole. It is important, therefore, that a key feature of nutrition education should deal with counteracting the results of decades of teaching aimed at reducing carbohydrate intakes.

Which brings us right to the F-Plan. The F-Plan is a *high*-carbohydrate diet, rich in the beneficial fibre-rich carbohydrate foods like unrefined cereals, fruit and vegetables. It is a low-fat diet. Most high-fibre foods are practically fat free. At the same time it moderates your intake of sugar. In fact it incorporates all the new major nutritional guidelines for weight control and health, with the possible exception of salt reduction (an excess of salt is now widely considered to be a health hazard). You can reduce salt intake while following the F-Plan just as easily as on any other pattern of eating. The question of timing is left to you simply because – realistically – those who attempt too many changes at once often find the task over-difficult. Give up smoking, shed that excess weight – but you will have a much greater chance of achieving both if you don't attempt the superhuman task of doing them both together. In the same way, the transitional period, during which you are concentrating on shedding weight and getting used to eating less fat and more fibre, may not be the ideal time to sacrifice your salt as well. You may prefer to wait until F-Plan eating has become effortlessly familiar before tackling the salt issue.

The F-Plan is NEWtrition – made realistic. It does not flinch at the sight of a supermarket can nor eschew a handily packaged slice of frozen haddock in favour of a rod and line. It pre-digests all the major new nutritional principles and serves them up as a plate of beans on toast. But *wholemeal* toast, if you please. And don't butter it.

It is not for extremists. It is for normal people who would like to be slim and would naturally prefer to protect themselves against the major health hazards if it is reasonably easy and practical to do so. The F-Plan – to the horror of the hair-shirt brigade – makes low-fat, high-fibre eating for weight control and health protection quite remarkably easy.

Prior to *The F-Plan* even health-conscious people aware of the increasing importance attached to dietary fibre intake found it difficult to know how to increase their intake sufficiently. Very few people knew which cereal, fruit and vegetable foods were the richest sources of dietary fibre. You would need a good deal of expertise to extract this information from a nutritional textbook, in which the information would be given only in terms of percentage of dietary fibre per hundred grams. This is rather a long stride from knowing that there is a useful quantity in an apple (2g), less in a stick of celery (1g) and a surprisingly large quantity (9g) in a small packet of frozen peas.

Many people believed that increasing dietary fibre intake simply meant sprinkling a bit of bran on almost everything. Not only does this require a certain masochism – an eat-your-hair-shirt (rather than wearing it) mentality – but it rarely provides you with a sufficient quantity of the stuff. Neither, unlike the F-Plan, does it follow the primary dietary-fibre rule for weight and health: increase your intake from a wide range of foods – cereals, fruits and vegetables.

The scientific research which has been reported during the two years since *The F-Plan* was published, has added even more emphasis to the F-Plan method of obtaining dietary fibre from a range of foods rather than from any single source. Much remains to be discovered about the effects on weight and health of this highly complex substance, but it is known that dietary fibre obtained from different foods has different effects on the body. It would appear, for instance, that cereal fibre is particularly helpful in speeding the elimination processes, while if fibre plays a part, as some scientists suspect, in lowering cholesterol levels, it seems likely that the dietary fibre present in fruit is of particular value in this.

Because the F-Plan is based on scientific facts and steers its followers into adhering to today's major nutritional guide-lines it has been warmly welcomed and supported by leaders of the medical and nutritional world; many general practitioners today recommend it to their patients both as a weight-reducing diet and as a realistic method of increasing fibre intake for preventing or treating health problems. The author is particularly indebted to those great pioneers of dietary-fibre research Dr Dennis Burkitt and Dr Hugh Trowell, who have been unfailingly generous in their encouragement and support. Not only that – by continuing to work with terrific energy in their seventies they add a splendid personal endorsement to their nutritional beliefs and fulfill the author's personal requirement of a good nutritionist: that he should live to a very ripe old age and finally have inscribed on his tombstone 'I told you so!'

Of today's younger pioneers in this field of research the author is particularly grateful to Dr David Southgate, whose analytical principles form the foundation of the most widely used methods for measuring dietary fibre, and who has been most kind and supportive. Without Derek Miller, eminent research scientist and lecturer in nutrition at London University, there would probably have been no F-Plan; the author's debt to him, for many years of teaching and friendship, is immeasurable.

A second quiet revolution that has been going on over the past years is the realization, on the part of the leaders of the medical and nutritional professions, that there is a need to communicate nutritional guide-lines to the public. No one has ever doubted the fact that the professional communicators of the media world are absolutely rotten at performing brain surgery. However, of late there has been increasing realization that a medical or scientific training is not necessarily ideal for learning the art of written communication. The F-Plan, which has measurably changed eating patterns in Britain in a remarkably short time, is a happy example of how progress can be speeded when medical and scientific experts and communicators work happily hand in hand.

Of course there have been a few critics. Those who seek to find a flaw usually seize on the fact that in seeking to increase dietary fibre intake in a modern, realistic way the F-Plan makes use of handy pre-packaged high-fibre foods like bran cereals and baked beans. And don't these – ha ha, caught you out – contain *SUGAR!*

Well yes, they do. And so do apples and pears and dates and grapes and lots of things made, not by Heinz or Crosse and Blackwell or Kelloggs, but by the Almighty. (It is always the policy of the author to turn for precedent to the very highest authority.)

In this age of excess weight in the Western world there can be no argument that we eat far too much sugar, which provides only calories – the things which make us fat – and none of the nutrients we need to keep our bodies functioning in a healthy way. Some nutritionists believe that our excessive intake of sugar contributes not only to obesity but to other health problems.

But it is not the inclusion of sugar in our diets which causes these problems, it is the inclusion of *enormous quantities* of sugar. In order to be slim and healthy we do not need to cut out all sugar, we need to cut out a good deal of sugar.

Which sugar? Well, it would seem reasonable that, for the sake of weight and health, we should first cut out those foods in which sugar is combined with nothing much that does us good and a good deal that does us harm. In many foods – chocolate, toffee, biscuits, cakes and many puddings – sugar is combined with fat, the most fattening of all foods, which we are also urged to restrict for the sake of our health. Obviously sugar-reduction should start with these doubly dangerous mega-baddies.

Next we come to foods and drinks which are more or less just neat or diluted sugar – sugar itself, sweet bottled and canned drinks, fat-free sweets like boiled sweets and mints and (sorry, health-food enthusiasts) honey. Clearly these are the next candidates for curtailment.

Thirdly, there is a category of foods in which sugar is combined with a good deal that is thought to do us good.

An example of such a food is canned baked beans in which sugar is used to add palatability to a rich source of vegetable protein, dietary fibre, and beneficial minerals and vitamins. Manufacturers: Heinz, Crosse and Blackwell, Tesco *et al.*

Further examples are apples, pears, oranges, carrots, etc., in which sugar adds palatability to useful sources of dietary fibre and beneficial minerals and vitamins. Manufacturer: Mother Nature.

Recent research, in which babies during the first hours of their lives showed a gratified expression (no, not a burp) when a sugar solution was put on their tongues, suggests that our liking for sweetness is a natural inbuilt predilection, not an acquired habit. It is the extraction of sugar from its natural sources, and so from its quantity-limiting association with dietary fibre, which would appear to be the root of the modern over-consumption problem.

When you follow the F-Plan you will consume considerably less sugar than you would on the average British diet, and the reduction will mainly be in the harmful (sugar-plus-fat) foods and the useless (sugar-plus-water) foods, rather than in those in which sugar is combined with dietary fibre and nutrients of value.

Talking of the burp, let us boldly mention a similar problem of greater social significance. To this criticism the F-Plan must openly plead guilty. If you switch from a low-fibre diet to one rich in vegetables ... well, er, yes, it can indeed happen. Take comfort from the fact that it is largely a temporary adjustment problem, go easy on the beans, which are the main offenders at the start, and cheer yourself with the thought that with two million F-Plan enthusiasts in Britain you are not alone with a flatulence problem.

These minor criticisms apart, it is somewhat difficult to criticize a diet which reverses all previous misconceptions about the most effective way to shed weight, provides a long-awaited, immeasurably better, new method, cuts down on the potentially harmful foods and increases intake of health-protective food in direct accord with the new nutritional guide-lines – and makes it all so EASY.

With this book you will find the F-Plan even easier. Happy slimming and good health!

Audrey Eyton

THE SECRET
OF THE F-PLAN

What the F-Plan does, which previous generations of slimming diets failed to do, is approximately to double your intake of substances called dietary fibre as it reduced your calorie intake. Dietary fibre is essentially the cell-wall material of plants. It is present in all cereal foods, fruits and vegetables, but some of these foods – wholemeal breads, bran cereals, strawberries, prunes, dates, peas, beans and sweetcorn, for instance – have a particularly high content. The F-Plan makes use of fibre-rich foods to increase intake of dietary fibre from the 15–20g a day usual in the British diet to 35–50g daily.

The fact that a generous intake of dietary fibre is helpful to those attempting to lose surplus fat is unarguable. That is a very bold claim to make in the field of nutrition where there are experts who will argue with almost anything. However, it is a claim which can be made with confidence, based on scientific evidence which either clearly proves or indicates that dietary fibre assists the slimmer not just in one way but in a whole variety of ways.

Argue the weight of scientific evidence against any one slimming benefit if you will, but you will still have to concede several other reasons why slimmers should increase their intake of dietary fibre. Any ONE of these reasons would provide sufficient reason for following the high-fibre path to weight loss. What would be totally unarguable, in light of the research of recent years, would be the case for a LOW-fibre diet (like the once-popular low-carbohydrate diet) for slimming. To follow any diet which does not provide a generous quantity of fibre-rich foods is to deprive yourself of a range of benefits which start the moment the food goes in to the mouth and continue right through the body to the final excretion process. These benefits have been revealed in detail in *The F-Plan*. However, here, for newcomers to the system, is a summary.

IN THE MOUTH

High-fibre foods provide you with a large bulk of food for a moderate quantity of calories. This, in itself, tends to lead towards a lower calorie consumption – but there are additional benefits for slimmers even before this food leaves the mouth. Fibre stimulates chewing, and scientific tests indicate that chewing promotes the sensation of satiety and fullness by a direct effect on the brain. The more you chew, the less you eat. Most overweight people eat considerably more quickly than slim people, and eating behaviour experts like psychiatrist Dr Henry Jordan regard slower eating as one of the most vital factors in weight reduction. If its only effect were to slow your eating, as it undoubtedly does, a high-fibre diet would probably have a long-term effect in reducing your weight, but this is just the beginning of its benefits.

IN THE STOMACH

High-fibre foods are the most filling foods of all. Dietary fibre is a sponge-like substance which absorbs water and actually swells up in the stomach. The benefits for the slimmer are obvious. On a high-fibre diet, as F-Plan dieters have discovered, you need never feel hungry, because not only is the food highly filling, it stays longer in the stomach than fibre-depleted food. When you are following a high-fibre diet you are taking a natural appetite suppressant as part of your food! Another reason why a high-fibre meal satisfies the appetite for longer than a typical Western fibre-depleted meal is associated with the blood sugar level. When blood sugar is low the body sends hunger signals to the brain, and this effect has been found to be particularly marked after meals based on low-fibre or fibre-free carbohydrate foods like sugar. However, a sufficient intake of dietary fibre solves this problem, adding a further long-term satiety bonus.

IN THE ELIMINATION PROCESSES

Dietary fibre speeds the elimination of waste matter, which provides well-documented health benefits and may also be partly responsible for the increase in speed of weight loss which can be achieved on a high-fibre diet. In various scientific tests an examination of the faeces of subjects following a high-fibre diet has shown them to contain more calories than is usual on a Westernized diet. One of the most recent tests, at London University's Department of Nutrition, indicates that this calorie wastage can be as high as 20 per cent on a high-fibre diet. This is a useful slimming bonus since the fewer calories your body uses from food, the more it must draw from its own surplus fat. Clearly more research needs to be done in this area, but it is probable that some high-fibre foods will prove to be more effective in this than others.

Meanwhile, more scientific evidence is emerging pointing to yet another reason why F-Plan dieting is speedier as well as easier than other methods. Recent research indicates that on a high-carbohydrate diet – and the F-Plan is a high-carbohydrate low-fat diet – the metabolic rate, which is the rate at which you burn up calories, is faster than when you follow an animal-food-based high-fat diet.

If you consume a thousand calories a day on the F-Plan, it seems that not only do some of them pass through undigested but also that the body may well be using up more calories than on other diets. So for your thousand-calorie-a-day diet you could be achieving (at this stage of research one can only guess the figures) a weight loss that you would expect to achieve on 900 calories a day on any other diet.

Consider all the scientific facts and indications and what the F-Plan adds up to, quite simply, is this: more weight loss for less willpower.

No wonder it has become the world's best-selling diet.

BASIC F-PLAN DIET RULES

There are a few essential rules which you should follow whichever F-Plan diet variation you choose to suit your life-style. These rules and the reason for them are outlined here to help you follow your chosen diet.

1. Determine your total daily calorie intake at a minimum of 1,000 and a maximum of 1,500. See p. 26 for guidance on your ideal dieting calorie total.

2. Aim to consume daily between 35g and 50g of dietary fibre. This level of dietary fibre intake ensures that you achieve the slimming benefits described in the introduction. This has been made easy for you when you follow any of the diets, since each menu has been planned to provide between 35g and 50g dietary fibre.

3. Ensure that you reach your daily dietary fibre target from a variety of foods and that you consume some of the most essential nutrients for a healthy diet by eating certain foods daily. These foods are referred to as the 'daily allowance' and are as follows:
● half a pint (285ml) of skimmed milk for adults and one pint (570ml) for children;
● two whole fresh fruits (an orange and an apple or pear);
● a daily portion of high-fibre cereal, usually Fibre-Filler (a type of home-made muesli). The ingredients and amounts are given on p. 24.
NB. Where the latter does not occur in the 'daily allowance' an alternative ready-packaged high-fibre breakfast cereal is included in the menu.

The total calories and fibre counts for the 'daily allowance' foods is given at the top of each menu and does not appear in the individual meals.

4. Apart from milk, sugarless tea and coffee (artificial sweeteners can be used), other drinks negligible in calories, e.g. water and low-calorie-labelled bottled and canned drinks, can be drunk at any time of day. No limit is set for these, but other drinks, especially

alcoholic drinks, must be cut out or strictly limited if your diet is to succeed, since they can provide a large number of calories. See p. 285 for further advice on alcoholic drinks.

Which of the following F-Plan diets you choose depends on your life-style – you may even decide that one diet suits you during the week and another at the weekends. As long as you choose a variety of menus for your chosen daily calorie intake you will be following a healthy weight-reducing diet.

FIBRE-FILLER

Fibre-Filler has been specially devised to provide a useful portion of your daily dietary fibre from cereal, fruit and nut sources. It has exceptional filling power and as such is a most valuable slimming aid. One daily portion of Fibre-Filler provides 15g of dietary fibre and 200 calories.

To make your daily quantity of Fibre-Filler, mix together the following ingredients:

For one day
½oz (15g) Bran Flakes
½oz (15g) bran
½oz (15g) All Bran or Bran Buds
¼oz (7g) almonds, chopped or flaked
¼oz (7g) dried prunes (just one large fruit) stoned and chopped
¼oz (7g) dried apricots, chopped
½oz (15g) sultanas

If you find it easier to multiply the ingredients and make several daily servings at one time you can do so but remember to mix the ingredients well since the bran tends to filter down to the bottom. To avoid this problem you could omit the bran and add ½oz (15g) bran to each daily portion after dividing up.

For eight days
4oz (115g) Bran Flakes
4oz (115g) bran
4oz (115g) All Bran or Bran Buds
2oz (55g) almonds, chopped or flaked

2oz (55g) dried prunes, stoned and chopped
2oz (55g) dried apricots, chopped
4oz (115g) sultanas

Divide into daily quantities and store in separate plastic storage bags.

A NOTE ON SUPPLEMENTS

Nutritional opinion is divided on whether those following a healthy slimming diet of varied food, like the F-Plan would benefit from a nutritional supplement. Some nutritionalists consider this unnecessary. Others argue that on a weight-shedding 1,000 calories a day, half the average woman's usual food intake, there is a greater chance of going short of nutrients. Those keeping to this lower calorie level for more than two or three weeks may choose to take a daily multi-vitamin pill with iron to provide a useful safeguard during their weight-losing period.

A NOTE ON MEASUREMENTS

Standard teaspoons, dessertspoons and tablespoons (5ml, 10ml and 15ml respectively) are used for these recipes. Unless otherwise indicated, a *level* spoonful should be used.

IMPERIAL/METRIC CONVERSION

In these diets and recipes, the conversions used have to be accurate so that the calorie and fibre quantities hold for both metric and imperial measurements. But as no cook would want to measure out quantities accurate to the nearest gram (226g, for example, for 8oz), these have been rounded to the nearest 5g (giving 225g for 8oz) in order to be more workable. The inaccuracy is minimal.

HOW MANY CALORIES?

The ready-planned F-Plan menus in this book provide either 1,500 or 1,250 or 1,000 calories a day. ALL overweight people will shed weight on 1,000 calories daily – it is scientifically impossible not to do so. Most dieters will shed weight on the upper level of 1,500 calories daily. Here is a guide to help you choose the ideal level for you.

1,500 Calorie Menus
All men can shed weight on 1,500 calories daily, but there is no reason why they should not follow the lower-calorie menus if they are aiming at a particularly rapid weight loss. Women who are more than two stone overweight and are at the start of a dieting campaign can also usually shed surplus weight quickly on 1,500 calories daily, particularly if they are tall or of medium height.

1,250 Calorie Menus
Combining a good speed of weight loss with a reasonably ample diet, this is the ideal calorie intake for most women dieters.

1,000 Calorie Menus
Women who have particular difficulty in shedding surplus weight at a satisfactory speed are recommended to keep to this lower level of calorie intake. Those mostly likely to come within this category are:

1. Those who are only a few pounds overweight;
2. Those who have already lost a good deal of weight and are in the later stages of a dieting campaign;
3. Small women.

Mixing Menus
Weight loss depends on average calorie intake over a period of time, rather than on precise daily calorie intake. So many dieters might find it a good plan to mix 1,500, 1,250 and 1,000 calorie menus throughout the week to fit in with their own pattern of life. For instance, if you find, as many slimmers do, that you can be stricter during the week than at weekends you might follow 1,000

calorie menus from Monday to Friday and then switch to 1,500 calorie menus on Saturdays and Sundays. On this pattern you would achieve the same weekly weight loss as you would on approximately 1,150 calories daily. On this averaging-out basis there is no reason why most dieters cannot freely draw on any diet menu in this book.

SIMPLY F-PLAN

The menus in this section provide the types of meals which have proved most popular with F-Plan dieters: plenty of nice ideas but never too much fuss or effort in shopping or cooking. The menus all follow the basic F-Plan rules (see p. 23) and are divided into three meals a day, plus a snack. All the meals are quick and simple to prepare and the foods are readily available.

The section is divided up into two parts; 1,000 calories and 1,250 calories daily, all providing 35–50g fibre. They are designed for a fast weight loss with the minimum of fuss.

SPECIAL DIET NOTES

1. Begin by deciding which daily calorie total will give you a satisfactory weight loss. You will find guidance on p. 26.

2. Select the menus from those of your chosen daily calorie total for one week at a time so that you can plan the shopping and always have the right foods available.

3. Vary the menus chosen to ensure that you eat a wide variety of foods.

4. Do *not* swap individual meals from one menu to another since all the menus have been carefully calorie and fibre calculated for a full day.

5. Make up the Fibre-Filler for your daily allowance either daily or for several days in one batch following the recipe on p. 24.

6. Allow yourself as much tea and coffee *without sugar* (sweeteners can be used) as you wish throughout the day *as long as* you use only the skimmed milk which remains from your daily allowance after you have had your Fibre-Filler. In addition you can drink as much water and drinks labelled 'low-calorie' as you wish. Alcoholic

drinks are not included in these menus; however, should you feel the need for an occasional alcoholic drink see the advice on alcoholic drinks on p. 285.

1,000 CALORIE MENU   1

	Calories	Fibre (g)
Daily allowance: Fibre-Filler (p. 24), ½ pint (285ml) skimmed milk, an orange and an apple or pear	400	20

Breakfast
Half portion of Fibre-Filler with milk from allowance

Lunch
* Pizza Toasts

An orange from allowance	325	8·5

Evening meal
1 packet frozen cod in butter or cheese sauce, cooked
4oz (115g) fresh or frozen peas, boiled
4oz (115g) carrots, boiled

An apple or pear from allowance	275	12·5

Snack
Remaining portion Fibre-Filler with milk from allowance

TOTAL	1,000	41

* Pizza Toasts

Serves 1

2 large thin slices (1½oz, 32g each) Hi-Bran bread
2 small tomatoes, sliced
salt and freshly ground pepper
¼ teaspoon dried thyme or mixed herbs
2oz (55g) Edam cheese, grated
2 stuffed olives, sliced

Toast the two slices of bread on both sides. Cover both slices of toast with the sliced tomatoes. Season well and sprinkle over the herbs. Top with the grated cheese and garnish with the slices of olive. Grill until the cheese is melted. Serve hot.

1,000 CALORIE MENU 2

	Calories	Fibre (g)
Daily allowance: Fibre-Filler (p. 24), ½ pint (285ml) skimmed milk, an orange and an apple or pear	400	20

Breakfast
Half portion of Fibre-Filler with milk from allowance

Lunch
4oz (115g) cottage cheese (natural or with chives or with onion and peppers or with pineapple) served with 3oz (85g) cooked beetroot, diced, mixed with 2oz (55g) mushrooms, sliced, 1 large stick celery, finely chopped, and 2 tablespoons oil-free French dressing
a few sprigs of watercress

| An apple or pear from allowance | 175 | 4·5 |

	Calories	Fibre (g)

Evening meal
* Baked Jacket Potato with Kidneys
2oz (55g) firm white cabbage, shredded
and tossed with 2 teaspoons oil-free
French dressing

	425	10·5

Snack
Remaining portion of Fibre-Filler with
milk from allowance

TOTAL	1,000	35

* Baked Jacket Potato with Kidneys

Serves 1

7oz (200g) potato
2 lamb's kidneys, skinned, core removed and chopped
1 small onion, chopped
4oz (115g) canned tomatoes, drained and chopped
4 tablespoons juice from canned tomatoes
dash of Worcestershire sauce
salt and pepper
1oz (30g, 1 rounded tablespoon) frozen peas

Scrub the potato well, then bake by one of the following methods:

1. Place the potato in the centre of a moderately hot oven (200°C, 400°F, gas 6) for 45 minutes or until soft when pinched.

2. Place the potato in a pan of water, bring to the boil, then simmer gently for 20 minutes. Drain. Place the potato in a moderately hot oven (190°C, 375°F, gas 5) for 10–15 minutes to crisp the skin.

3. Prick well all over and cook in a microwave oven on full power for 4 minutes, turning after 2 minutes.

Meanwhile place the lamb's kidneys, onion, canned tomatoes and juice in a small pan. Add the Worcestershire sauce and salt and pepper. Heat to boiling point, cover and simmer gently for 15 minutes. Stir in the peas and heat through. Cut the baked potato in half lengthwise and scoop out some of the flesh. Mix it with the hot kidney mixture and pile back into the potato jacket. Serve with shredded white cabbage.

1,000 CALORIE MENU 3

	Calories	Fibre (g)
Daily allowance: Fibre-Filler (p. 24), ½ pint (285ml) skimmed milk, an orange and an apple or pear	400	20
Breakfast Half portion Fibre-Filler with milk from allowance		
Lunch * Kidney Bean Soup 1 large thin slice (1¼oz. 32g) Hi-Bran bread		
An apple or pear from allowance	190	14
Evening meal * Cheese and Sweetcorn Omelet 1 average-sized tomato, fresh or grilled without fat		
150g carton low-fat natural yogurt with orange from allowance and artificial sweetener, if necessary	410	4
Snack Remaining portion Fibre-Filler with milk from allowance		
TOTAL	1,000	38

* Kidney Bean Soup

Serves 1

4oz (115g) canned red kidney beans, drained
1oz (30g) chopped onion
1 large stick celery, chopped
7½fl oz (215ml) beef stock made from ½ beef stock cube
1 bay leaf
salt and pepper
¼ teaspoon chilli powder

Put all the ingredients in a saucepan. Bring to the boil, cover and simmer for 30 minutes. Remove the bay leaf and serve the soup as it is, or purée in a blender if preferred.

* Cheese and Sweetcorn Omelet

Serves 1

2 eggs (size 3)
salt and pepper
a dash of Worcestershire sauce
¼oz (7g) low-fat spread
2oz (55g) canned sweetcorn, drained
1oz (30g) green pepper, finely chopped
1oz (30g) Edam cheese, grated

Beat the eggs, 2 tablespoons water, seasoning and Worcestershire sauce together. Grease a non-stick omelet pan with the low-fat spread and heat. Pour in the eggs and cook gently until almost set. Sprinkle over the sweetcorn, green pepper and grated cheese. Heat under the grill until the cheese begins to melt. Fold the omelet and serve.

1,000 CALORIE MENU 4

	Calories	Fibre (g)
Daily allowance: Fibre-Filler (p. 24), ½ pint (285ml) skimmed milk, an orange and an apple or pear	400	20

	Calories	Fibre (g)

Breakfast
Half portion of Fibre-Filler with milk from
allowance

Lunch
8oz (225g) canned baked beans in tomato
sauce, heated and served on 1 large thin
slice (1⅛oz, 32g) Hi-Bran bread, toasted and
garnished with 1 average-sized tomato, cut
into wedges

An orange from allowance	235	20·5

Evening meal
1 bacon steak (3½oz, 100g raw weight),
grilled
3½oz (100g) canned pease pudding
4oz (115g) Brussels sprouts, boiled

2oz (55g) vanilla ice-cream	365	8·5

Snack
Remaining portion Fibre-Filler with milk
from allowance

An apple or pear from allowance

TOTAL	1,000	49

1,000 CALORIE MENU **5**

	Calories	Fibre (g)
Daily allowance: Fibre-Filler (p. 24), ½ pint (285ml) skimmed milk, an orange and an apple or pear	400	20

	Calories	Fibre (g)

Breakfast
Half portion of Fibre-Filler with milk from
allowance

An orange from allowance

Lunch
* Tuna Salad Sandwich

An apple or pear from allowance   250   7

Evening meal
8oz (225g) (raw weight) chicken leg joint,
grilled and skin removed
6oz (170g) potato, baked in its jacket
(p. 31) with 1 tablespoon oil-free French
dressing
2 oz (55g) fresh or frozen peas, boiled   350   9

Snack
Remaining portion Fibre-Filler with milk
from allowance

TOTAL	1,000	36

* Tuna Salad Sandwich

Serves 1

2 large thin slices (1½oz, 35g each) wholemeal bread
1 tablespoon low-calorie salad dressing
2oz (55g) tuna, canned in brine, flaked
1 lettuce leaf
1 tomato, sliced
a few slices of cucumber

Spread both slices of bread with the salad dressing and fill with the
remaining ingredients.

1,000 CALORIE MENU 6

	Calories	Fibre (g)
Daily allowance: Fibre-Filler (p. 24), ½ pint (285ml) skimmed milk, an orange and an apple or pear	400	20

Breakfast
Half portion Fibre-Filler with milk from allowance

An orange from allowance

Lunch
2 Energen F-Plan Diet Brancrisps, topped with 2oz (55g) cottage cheese, natural, mixed with ½oz (15g) stoned dates, chopped, and ½oz (15g) shelled walnuts, chopped

	Calories	Fibre (g)
1 large stick celery, cut into pieces		
An apple or pear from allowance	210	5·5

Evening meal
	Calories	Fibre (g)
* Egg Florentine		
* Poached Citrus Plums	390	12

Snack
Remaining portion of Fibre-Filler with milk from allowance

	Calories	Fibre (g)
TOTAL	1,000	37·5

* Egg Florentine

Serves 1

5oz (140g) frozen cut-leaf spinach, thawed
1 egg (size 3)

2½oz (70g) natural low-fat yogurt
¼ teaspoon prepared mustard
salt and pepper
½oz (15g) Cheddar cheese, grated
½oz (15g) wholemeal breadcrumbs

Heat the thawed spinach gently (without adding butter) in a small
pan or in a microwave oven, then spoon into the bottom of a small
fireproof dish. Poach the egg and place on top of the spinach.
Blend the yogurt with the made mustard and seasoning to taste,
and spoon over the egg. Mix the grated cheese and breadcrumbs
and sprinkle over the top. Heat under a grill until the topping is
crisp and brown.

* Poached Citrus Plums

Serves 1

4oz (115g) sweet plums
4 tablespoons fresh orange juice
1 level teaspoon sugar (optional)
1 level dessertspoon flaked almonds

Wash the plums and place in a pan with the orange juice. Cover
with a tight-fitting lid and heat gently for 5 minutes. Add the
sugar, if liked. Serve hot or cold sprinkled with the flaked almonds.

1,000 CALORIES MENU 7

	Calories	Fibre (g)
Daily allowance: Fibre-Filler (p. 24), ½ pint (285ml) skimmed milk, an orange and an apple or pear	400	20

Breakfast
Half portion Fibre-Filler with milk from
allowance

An orange from allowance

	Calories	Fibre (g)

Lunch
* Lentil and Vegetable Soup
2 Energen F-Plan Diet Brancrisps

| An apple or pear from allowance | 220 | 10·5 |

Evening meal
3oz (85g) sliced lean boiled ham served with
* Coleslaw and 2 average-sized tomatoes,
sliced
A bunch of watercress
A few cucumber slices
A few lettuce leaves
1 large thin slice (1½oz, 35g) wholemeal
bread spread with ½oz (7g) low-fat spread

| 4oz (115g) green grapes | 380 | 10·5 |

Snack
Remaining portion Fibre-Filler with milk
from allowance

| **TOTAL** | 1,000 | 41 |

* Lentil and Vegetable Soup

Serves 1 (several portions can be made at one time and frozen until required)

1½oz (45g) red lentils
1oz (30g) onion, chopped
2oz (55g) carrot, sliced
1 large stick celery, chopped
1 chicken or ham stock cube, dissolved in ¾ pint (425ml) boiling
  water
salt and pepper

Put all the ingredients in a pan. Bring to the boil, cover and simmer gently for 1 hour.

* Coleslaw

Serves 1

3oz (85g) firm white cabbage, shredded
1 level tablespoon finely chopped onion
2oz (55g) carrot, grated
2 tablespoons oil-free French dressing

Mix the cabbage, onion and carrot together. Add the dressing and toss well.

1,000 CALORIE MENU **8**

	Calories	Fibre (g)
Daily allowance: Fibre-Filler, (p. 24), ½ pint (285ml) skimmed milk, an orange and an apple or pear	400	20
Breakfast Half portion of Fibre-Filler with milk from allowance		
Lunch * Crunchy Sardine Sandwich An apple or pear from allowance	235	6·5
Evening meal * Baked Jacket Potato with Chicken Liver Filling 2oz (55g) runner beans, boiled An orange from allowance	365	9
Snack Remaining portion Fibre-Filler with milk from allowance		
TOTAL	1,000	35·5

* Crunchy Sardine Sandwich

Serves 1
2 large thin slices (1½oz, 35g each) wholemeal bread
1 tablespoon low-calorie salad dressing
1 sardine in tomato sauce
1oz (30g) raw bean sprouts
1 tablespoon chopped green pepper

Spread the bread with the salad dressing. Mash the sardine and spread on one slice of bread. Top with bean sprouts and green pepper and the second slice of bread. Cut into four sandwiches.

* Baked Jacket Potato with Chicken Liver Filling

Serves 1

7oz (200g) potato
4oz (115g) chicken livers, chopped
1oz (30g) finely chopped onion
1oz (30g) canned sweetcorn
salt and pepper
1 level teaspoon tomato purée

Bake the potato following one of the methods on p. 31. Place the chicken livers, onion, sweetcorn and 4 tablespoons water in a small pan. Add the salt, pepper and tomato purée. Heat to simmering point, cover and simmer gently for 5 minutes. Cut the potato in half lengthwise and scoop out some of the flesh. Mix with the chicken liver mixture and pile back into the potato jacket. Serve at once.

1,000 CALORIE MENU   9

	Calories	Fibre (g)
Daily allowance: Fibre-Filler (p. 24), ½ pint (285ml) skimmed milk, an orange and an apple or pear	400	20

	Calories	Fibre (g)

Breakfast
Half portion Fibre-Filler with milk from
allowance

Lunch
* Mushroom and Tomato Scramble on Toast

An orange from allowance	325	9

Evening meal
6oz (170g) cod or haddock fillets, brushed
with ¼oz (7g) low-fat spread and grilled
4oz (115g) peas, boiled
2oz (55g) raw bean sprouts, blanched
4oz (115g) canned tomatoes, heated

5½oz (155g) banana	275	13·5

Snack
Remaining portion Fibre-Filler with milk
from allowance

TOTAL	1,000	42·5

* **Mushroom and Tomato Scramble on Toast**

Serves 1

2 large thin slices (1⅛oz, 32g each) Hi-Bran bread
2fl oz (55ml) skimmed milk, additional to allowance
2oz (55g) mushrooms, sliced
2 eggs (size 3)
salt and pepper
1 average-sized tomato, chopped
1 tablespoon chopped parsley (optional)

Toast both sides of bread. Put the milk and mushrooms in a pan. Heat gently for 3 minutes. Beat the eggs with the seasoning and stir into the mushrooms. Cook, stirring continuously until the eggs are creamy. Stir in the chopped tomato. Top the two slices of toast with the mushroom and tomato scramble. Sprinkle with chopped parsley, if liked.

1,000 CALORIE MENU   10

	Calories	Fibre (g)
Daily allowance: Fibre-Filler (p. 24), ½ pint (285ml) skimmed milk, an orange and an apple or pear	400	20
Breakfast Half portion of Fibre-Filler with milk from allowance		
An orange from allowance		
Lunch * Creamy Spinach Soup 2 Energen F-Plan Diet Brancrisps		
An apple or pear from allowance	175	11·5
Evening meal * Savoury Mince Half a medium packet Smash Potato Pieces made up with boiling water, no butter 4 oz (115g) Brussels sprouts, boiled		
2oz (55g) blackberries stewed with 4oz (115g) cooking apple, peeled, cored and sliced, 2 tablespoons water and 1½ teaspoons sugar	425	18

	Calories	Fibre (g)

Snack
Remaining portion Fibre-Filler with milk
from allowance

TOTAL	1,000	49·5

* Creamy Spinach Soup

Serves 1 (several portions can be made up at one time and frozen until required)

5oz (140g) frozen cut-leaf spinach, thawed
7½fl oz (215ml) skimmed milk (additional to allowance)
3 level teaspoons Mornflake Oatbran and Oatgerm *or* fine oatmeal
salt and pepper
grated nutmeg

Put the spinach, milk and Oatbran and Oatgerm or fine oatmeal in a pan. Bring to the boil and simmer for 3 minutes. Purée in a blender and season to taste with salt, pepper and grated nutmeg.

* Savoury Mince

Serves 1

4oz (115g) lean minced beef
1 small onion, peeled and finely chopped
1 stick celery, finely chopped
¼ beef stock cube, dissolved in 2½ oz (70ml) boiling water
salt and pepper
pinch of mixed herbs
1 level teaspoon tomato purée
1oz (30g) frozen peas

Fry the minced beef in a non-stick saucepan until well browned. Drain off all the fat which runs out of the meat. Add the onion, celery and stock to the meat in the pan and bring to the boil, stirring. Reduce the heat, season to taste with salt and pepper and add the herbs and tomato purée and stir. Cover and simmer for 30 minutes. stirring occasionally and adding more water if it begins to boil dry. Stir in the peas and heat through for 5 minutes.

1,250 CALORIE MENU   1

	Calories	Fibre (g)
Daily allowance: Fibre-Filler (p. 24), ½ pint (285ml) skimmed milk, an orange and an apple or pear	400	20

Breakfast
Half portion Fibre-Filler with milk from allowance

1 large thin slice (1¼oz, 32g) Hi-Bran bread, spread with ¼oz (7g) low-fat spread and 1 level teaspoon honey or marmalade	105	3·5

Lunch
* Corned Beef and Baked Bean Sandwich

2oz (55g) raw carrot sticks

An apple or pear from allowance	235	10·5

Evening meal
* Ham and Pepper Omelet
4oz (115g) frozen mixed vegetables, boiled

8oz (225g) can Koo Peach Slices in Apple Juice		
1½oz (45g) vanilla ice-cream	510	8·5

	Calories	Fibre (g)

Snack

Remaining portion Fibre-Filler with milk
from allowance

An orange from allowance

	Calories	Fibre (g)
TOTAL	1,250	42·5

---

* Corned Beef and Baked Bean Sandwich

Serves 1

2 large thin slices (1½oz, 32g each) Hi-Bran bread
1 tablespoon tomato sauce
1oz (30g) corned beef
1oz (30g) canned baked beans in tomato sauce
pepper
a few slices of cucumber

Spread the slices of bread with the tomato sauce. Mash the corned beef with the baked beans and pepper to taste. Spread over one slice of the bread. Top with cucumber slices and cover with the second slice of bread. Cut into four sandwiches.

---

* Ham and Pepper Omelet

Serves 1

2 eggs (size 3)
salt and pepper
¼oz (7g) low-fat spread
2oz (55g) boiled lean ham, chopped
1½oz (45g) chopped green pepper

Beat the eggs with 2 tablespoons water and salt and pepper to taste. Grease a non-stick omelet pan with the low-fat spread and heat. Pour in the egg mixture and cook gently until almost set.

Sprinkle over the chopped ham and green pepper and heat under the grill for 1 minute. Fold the omelet and serve.

1,250 CALORIE MENU 2

	Calories	Fibre (g)
Daily allowance: Fibre-Filler (p. 24), ½ pint (285ml) skimmed milk, an orange and an apple or pear	400	20
Breakfast		
Half portion Fibre-Filler with milk from allowance		
1 large thin slice (1¼oz, 35g) wholemeal bread, toasted and spread with ¼oz (7g) low-fat spread	100	3
Lunch		
2 Energen F-Plan Diet Brancrisps, spread with 1oz (30g) peanut butter and topped with 1 tomato, sliced, a few slices cucumber and ½ carton of mustard and cress		
An average-sized banana (6oz, 170g)	315	9
Evening meal		
* Frankfurter Salad		
150g carton low-fat fruit-flavoured yogurt		
An apple or pear from allowance	435	9
Snack		
Remaining portion Fibre-Filler with milk from allowance		
TOTAL	1,250	41

* Frankfurter Salad

Serves 1

7½oz (215g) can butter beans, drained
2oz (55g) frankfurter, sliced
1 small green pepper, seeds removed and chopped
1oz (30g) radishes, sliced
2–3 spring onions, chopped
3 tablespoons oil-free French dressing
a few lettuce leaves

Put the butter beans, frankfurter, green pepper, radishes and spring onions into a bowl. Add the French dressing and toss well. Serve on a bed of lettuce leaves.

1,250 CALORIE MENU   **3**

	Calories	Fibre (g)
Daily allowance: Fibre-Filler (p. 24), ½ pint (285ml) skimmed milk, an orange and an apple or pear	400	20
Breakfast Half portion of Fibre-Filler with milk from allowance		
Lunch * Bean and Ham Toppers An orange from allowance	330	21
Evening meal * Macaroni Cheese 5oz (140g) green grapes	520	9
Snack Remaining portion Fibre-Filler with milk from allowance		

	Calories	Fibre (g)
An apple or pear from allowance		
TOTAL	1,250	50

* Bean and Ham Toppers

Serves 1

1 wholemeal round bread roll (2oz, 55g)
½ teaspoon made mustard
8oz (225g) canned baked beans in tomato sauce
1oz (30g) boiled lean ham, chopped

Split the bread roll and spread both cut surfaces with the mustard. Heat the baked beans and pile on top of the two halves of the bread roll. Sprinkle the chopped ham over the beans and serve.

* Macaroni Cheese

Serves 1

2oz (55g) wholewheat macaroni
½oz (15g) wholemeal flour
¼ pint (140ml) skimmed milk (additional to allowance)
¼oz (7g) low-fat spread
salt and pepper
¼ teaspoon made mustard
1oz (30g) Cheddar cheese, grated
1 average-sized tomato, sliced

Boil the macaroni in salted water for 12 minutes or until tender; drain. Put the flour, milk and low-fat spread into a saucepan and heat, whisking continuously until it boils and thickens. Season to taste with salt and pepper. Add the mustard and half the cheese. Stir the macaroni into the sauce. Pour into an ovenproof dish. Top with the tomato slices and the remaining grated cheese.

Heat under the grill until the cheese is melted and beginning to brown.

1,250 CALORIE MENU 4

	Calories	Fibre (g)
Daily allowance: Fibre-Filler (p. 24), ½ pint (285ml) skimmed milk, an orange and an apple or pear	400	20

Breakfast
Half portion of Fibre-Filler with milk from allowance

Lunch
* Mushrooms and Sweetcorn on Toast

1 Jordans Original Crunchy Bar, Honey & Coconut

An apple or pear from allowance	345	8·5

Evening meal
* Sardine Salad
8oz (225g) potato, baked in its jacket (see p. 31 for baking instructions) topped with 2 tablespoons low-fat natural yogurt mixed with 1 teaspoon tomato purée and salt and pepper to taste

An orange from allowance	505	12

Snack
Remaining portion Fibre-Filler with milk from allowance

TOTAL	1,250	40·5

* Mushrooms and Sweetcorn on Toast

Serves 1

1 large thin slice (1½oz, 35g) wholemeal bread
2oz (55g) button mushrooms
4fl oz (115ml) skimmed milk (additional to allowance)
2 teaspoons cornflour
1 tablespoon low-fat natural yogurt
2oz (55g) canned sweetcorn
salt and pepper
a dash of Worcestershire sauce

Toast the bread on both sides. Poach the mushrooms in 3fl oz (85ml) of the milk for 5 minutes. Blend the cornflour with the remaining milk and stir into the mushrooms. Bring to the boil, stirring, and cook for 2 minutes until thickened. Add the yogurt and sweetcorn. Season to taste with salt and pepper and stir in the Worcestershire sauce. Heat gently for 2 minutes. Serve the mushrooms and sweetcorn mixture on the toast.

* Sardine Salad

Serves 1

4½oz (130g) canned sardines in tomato sauce
a few lettuce leaves
2 large sticks celery, chopped
2oz (55g) carrot, grated
2oz (55g) fresh garden peas or thawed frozen peas
1 tablespoon oil-free French dressing

Arrange the sardines on the lettuce leaves. Mix the celery, carrot and peas with the French dressing and serve with the sardines.

1,250 CALORIE MENU   **5**

	Calories	Fibre (g)
Daily allowance: Fibre-Filler (p. 24), ½ pint (285ml) skimmed milk, an orange and an apple or pear	400	20

	Calories	Fibre (g)

Breakfast
Half portion of Fibre-Filler with milk from
allowance

1 large thin slice (1¼oz, 35g) wholemeal bread, toasted and spread with ¼oz (7g) low-fat spread and 2 level teaspoons honey or marmalade	130	3

Lunch
1 egg (size 3). hard-boiled. served with a
few lettuce leaves. a small bunch of
watercress, 2oz (55g) grated carrot mixed
with ½oz (15g) raisins, a few radishes and
spring onions and 1 tablespoon low-calorie
salad dressing

150g carton low-fat fruit-flavoured yogurt	285	4·5

Evening meal
* Grilled Lamb Chop with Savoury Topping
4oz (115g) fresh or frozen peas. boiled
3oz (85g) carrots, boiled

An orange from allowance	435	14·5

Snack
Remaining portion Fibre-Filler with milk
from allowance

An apple or pear from allowance

TOTAL	1,250	42

* **Grilled Lamb Chop with Savoury Topping**

Serves 1

1 lamb loin chop (5oz, 140g raw weight)

1 small onion, sliced
4oz (115g) canned tomatoes, chopped
salt and pepper
a dash of Worcestershire sauce
½oz (15g) wholemeal breadcrumbs
a generous pinch of dried mixed herbs

Grill the lamb chop until cooked through. Meanwhile heat the sliced onion, canned tomatoes, salt and pepper together in a pan for 5 minutes, or until the onion is softened. Put half the onion and tomato mixture in a small heatproof dish. Put the grilled lamb chop on top and spoon over the remaining onion and tomato mixture. Mix the breadcrumbs with the mixed herbs and sprinkle evenly over the top of the chop. Heat under the grill until the breadcrumbs are crisp and browned.

1,250 CALORIE MENU 6

	Calories	Fibre (g)
Daily allowance: Fibre-Filler (p. 24), ½ pint (285 ml) skimmed milk, an orange and an apple or pear	400	20
Breakfast		
Half portion Fibre-Filler with milk from allowance		
1 Ryvita crispbread, brown or original, spread with 1 level teaspoon honey or marmalade (no butter)	40	1
Lunch		
* Crunchy Salad with Ham		
2 Ryvita crispbreads, brown or original, spread with ¼oz (7g) low-fat spread		
An orange from allowance	260	10

	Calories	Fibre (g)
Evening meal 2 pork sausages (2oz, 55g each), grilled 1 average-sized tomato, halved, grilled without fat 8oz (225g) canned baked beans in tomato sauce, 5oz (140g) boiled potatoes, mashed, using skimmed milk from allowance and no butter *or* half medium packet Smash Potato Pieces, made up without butter	550	19
Snack Remaining portion Fibre-Filler with milk from allowance An apple or pear from allowance		
TOTAL	1,250	50

* Crunchy Salad with Ham

Serves 1

4oz (115g) red cabbage, shredded
1 carrot, grated
1 leek (green part removed), thinly sliced
1 tablespoon oil-free French dressing
1 tablespoon low-calorie salad dressing
2oz (55g) boiled lean ham, sliced

Mix the red cabbage, carrot and leek together. Add the French
dressing and salad dressing and toss well until thoroughly blended.
Serve with the slices of ham.

1,250 CALORIE MENU   7

	Calories	Fibre (g)
Daily allowance: Fibre-Filler (p. 24), ½ pint (285ml) skimmed milk, an orange and an apple or pear	400	20

	Calories	Fibre (g)
Breakfast Half portion Fibre-Filler with milk from allowance		
1 egg (size 3), poached and served on 1 large thin slice (1½oz, 35g) wholemeal bread, toasted	155	3
Lunch * Cauliflower Soup 2 Energen F-Plan Diet Brancrisps, spread with ½oz (7g) low-fat spread		
1 apple or pear from allowance	155	6·5
Evening meal 2 bacon steaks (3½oz, 100g each), grilled without added fat, served with 2 pineapple rings, canned in natural juice, grilled 3oz (85g) canned sweetcorn 4oz (115g) runner beans, boiled 2 Energen F-Plan Diet Brancrisps, spread with ½oz (7g) low-fat spread and served with 1oz (30g) Edam cheese and 1 large stick celery	540	12·5
Snack Remaining portion Fibre-Filler with milk from allowance		
TOTAL	1,250	42

* Cauliflower Soup

Serves 1

6oz (170g) cauliflower, broken into florets

1oz (30g) onion, chopped
½ chicken stock cube
1 level tablespoon dried skimmed milk powder
salt and pepper
2 level teaspoons grated Parmesan cheese

Put the cauliflower and onion into a small saucepan. Dissolve the stock cube in ½ pint (285ml) boiling water and add to the pan. Cook until the vegetables are tender, about 15–20 minutes. Sieve or purée the soup in a blender. Return to the pan. Beat in the dried skimmed milk and season to taste with salt and pepper. Reheat gently. Serve topped with the Parmesan cheese.

1,250 CALORIE MENU 8

This menu is suitable for vegetarians

	Calories	Fibre (g)
Daily allowance: Fibre-Filler (p. 24), ½ pint (285ml) skimmed milk, an orange and an apple or pear	400	20
Breakfast Half portion of Fibre-Filler with milk from allowance		
1 egg (size 3), boiled and served with 1 Ryvita crispbread, brown or original, spread with ¼oz (7g) low-fat spread	130	1
Lunch 2oz (55g) flat round wholemeal roll (bap), split and filled with 1oz (30g) peanut butter, 2oz (55g) grated carrot and 1 lettuce leaf		
An orange from allowance	305	8·5

	Calories	Fibre (g)
Evening meal		
* Ratatouille au Gratin		
4oz (115g) fresh or frozen raspberries or strawberries		
1oz (30g) vanilla ice-cream	415	19·5/ 13·5
Snack		
Half portion Fibre-Filler with milk from allowance		
TOTAL	1,250	49/43

* Ratatouille au Gratin

Serves 1

1 small aubergine (6oz, 170g)
salt and pepper
1 medium onion (3oz, 85g), peeled and sliced
1 courgette (5oz, 140g), sliced
2 average-sized tomatoes, sliced
½ teaspoon dried mixed herbs
2oz (55g) Edam cheese, grated
1 large thin slice (1¼oz, 35g) wholemeal bread

Slice the aubergine into ¼ inch (6mm) slices. Sprinkle the cut surfaces with salt, then leave to stand for 30 minutes to draw out the juices. Rinse the aubergine, drain and dry. Put aubergine slices, onion, courgette, tomatoes and mixed herbs in an ovenproof dish. Season to taste with salt and pepper. Sprinkle the grated cheese on top of the vegetables. Bake at 180°C (350°F, gas 4) for 30 minutes, until the vegetables are tender. Serve with the bread to mop up the juices.

1,250 CALORIE MENU 9

This menu is suitable for vegetarians

	Calories	Fibre (g)
Daily allowance: Fibre-Filler (p. 24), ½ pint (285ml) skimmed milk, an orange and an apple or pear	400	20

Breakfast
Half portion Fibre-Filler with milk from allowance

An average-sized banana (6oz, 170g)	80	3·5

Lunch
* Cheese and Apple Sandwich

150g carton low-fat fruit-flavoured yogurt	365	7

Evening meal
* Layered Bean Casserole

An orange from allowance	325	19·5

Snack
Remaining portion Fibre-Filler with milk from allowance

A cup of chocolate, made up from 1 rounded teaspoon drinking chocolate and 6fl oz (170ml) skimmed milk, additional to allowance	80	0

TOTAL	1,250	50

* **Cheese and Apple Sandwich**

Serves 1

1 tablespoon low-calorie salad dressing
1oz (30g) Edam cheese, grated
2 large thin slices (1½oz, 32g each) Hi-Bran bread
eating apple from allowance

Mix the salad dressing with the grated cheese and spread over both
slices of bread. Cut the apple in half. Core one half and then slice
thinly. Arrange the apple slices over one of the cheese-covered
slices of bread and top with the second slice of bread. Cut into four
sandwiches. Cut the remaining half apple into wedges and eat
with the sandwich.

* **Layered Bean Casserole**

Serves 1

2oz (55g) canned red kidney beans, drained
7½oz (215g) canned butter beans, drained
6oz (170g) canned tomatoes, chopped
1oz (30g) finely chopped onion
salt and pepper
pinch of dried basil
4½oz (130g) canned chopped-leaf spinach, drained
grated nutmeg
1 small packet (25g) crisps, any flavour, crushed

Spoon the red kidney beans into the bottom of a small ovenproof
casserole. Cover with the butter beans. Mix the tomatoes with the
onion, salt, pepper and basil, and spoon over the beans. Spread the
spinach over the top and sprinkle on a little grated nutmeg. Cover
and bake at 190°C (375°F, gas 5) for 35 minutes. Uncover and
sprinkle over the crushed crisps. Return to the oven for 5 minutes,
uncovered. Serve hot.

1,250 CALORIES MENU   10

This menu is suitable for vegetarians

	Calories	Fibre (g)
Daily allowance: Fibre-Filler (p. 24), ½ pint (285ml) skimmed milk, an orange and an apple or pear	400	20

Breakfast
Whole portion Fibre-Filler with milk from
allowance

Lunch
7½oz (215g) canned spaghetti in tomato
sauce, heated and covered with 1 sliced
tomato and ½oz (15g) grated Edam
cheese

An apple or pear from allowance   195   3

Evening meal
* Vegetable Paella

Fruit salad made with 2oz (55g) grapes,
1 orange from allowance, segmented,
1 average-sized banana (6oz, 170g), sliced,
and 2fl oz (55ml) apple juice   545   16

Snack
150g carton low-fat natural yogurt with
2 teaspoons clear honey   110   0

| **TOTAL** | 1,250 | 39 |

* Vegetable Paella

Serves 1

2oz (55g) brown long-grain rice
1 small onion, chopped
1 small green pepper (4oz, 115g), seeds removed and chopped
2 average-sized tomatoes, chopped
1oz (30g) mushrooms, sliced
1oz (30g) fresh or frozen peas
$\frac{1}{4}$ teaspoon dried thyme or marjoram
$\frac{1}{2}$ teaspoon grated lemon rind
salt and pepper
1oz (30g) roasted peanuts or cashew nuts

Put the rice, onion, pepper, tomatoes, mushrooms, peas, 8fl oz (225ml) boiling water and herbs into a saucepan. Bring to the boil, stir well and cover and simmer gently for about 25 minutes until the rice is tender. Add more water during cooking if the rice mixture becomes too dry. Stir in the grated lemon rind and salt and pepper to taste. Turn out on a serving dish and sprinkle the nuts over the top.

F-PLAN FOR
WORKING WOMEN

All the menus in this section include a packable lunch, making them ideal for women who are out at work all day. The easiest and often the only way to stick to your diet when you have to eat lunch at work is to take your own meal with you. Those who think that packed lunches must always be sandwiches will be pleasantly surprised to find that the lunches given here also include salads, soups, crispbreads with toppings, pizza and filled rolls. All are easy to pack and eat, as long as you remember to pack any necessary items of cutlery. Hot soups can easily be carried in a thermos flask; only ready prepared canned soups have been included since working women do not have time to cook home-made soups before leaving for work in the morning, and it is unwise to keep home-made soup warm in a thermos flask from the previous evening.

The meals for the rest of the day in each menu are breakfast (either Fibre-Filler or Energen F-Plan Crunchy Bran Muesli), evening meal (usually something quick and easy since most working people have little time for meal preparation after work) and a snack which can be eaten any time during the evening.

The menus are divided into two sections of 1,000 and 1,250 calories. Half the menus in each section contain Fibre-Filler in the daily allowance as in all basic F-Plan diets and the remaining menus contain Energen F-Plan Crunchy Bran Muesli in the daily allowance so that you can decide which suits you best or use both, on different days, to provide variety.

While the menus with the packed lunches are just right for weekdays or working days you might like to have something different at the weekend. You will find plenty of choice for weekend menus in the 'Simply F-Plan' (p. 28) and the 'Keen Cooks F-Plan' (p. 119) menus.

SPECIAL DIET NOTES

1. Decide on your daily calorie allowance, either 1,000 calories or 1,250 calories, which will depend on how fast you want your

weight loss to be, how overweight you are and the amount of physical work you do.

2. Include as many different menus as possible from the selection provided, to keep your diet interesting and nutritious.

3. Do not swap individual meals from one menu to another since all the menus have been carefully calorie and fibre counted.

4. Drink as much sugarless tea and coffee as you like, either black or with the skimmed milk which remains from your daily allowance after using it on the Fibre-Filler or muesli. You can use artificial sweeteners. In addition you can drink unlimited amounts of canned and bottled low-calorie labelled drinks (e.g. Tab, Diet Pepsi Cola, Low-Calorie Bitter Lemon) and also water and soda water. In fact it is often helpful to have a low-calorie fizzy drink when your willpower is flagging, since such drinks can make you feel full. Alcoholic drinks have not been included in these menus. However, there may be occasions when you feel you must have an alcoholic drink; in this case, select a 1,000-calorie menu and allow yourself drinks to the value of 200 or 250 calories from the chart on p. 285.

1,000 CALORIE MENU   1

	Calories	Fibre (g)
Daily allowance: Fibre-Filler (p. 24), ½ pint (285ml) skimmed milk, an orange and an apple or pear	400	20

Breakfast
Half portion of Fibre-Filler with milk from allowance

Office or work lunch
* Sardine and Cucumber Sandwich

2oz (55g) carrot sticks
1 large stick celery, cut into short sticks

| An apple or pear from allowance | 225 | 8·5 |

	Calories	Fibre (g)

Evening meal

1 chicken leg joint (8oz, 225g raw weight),
grilled and then skin removed
4oz (115g) canned sweetcorn
4oz (115g) mushrooms, poached in a little
stock, *or* 7½oz (215g) canned button
mushrooms in brine, heated

2oz (55g) vanilla ice-cream served with		
orange from allowance, segmented, and		
1oz (30g) black grapes	375	9·5

Suppertime snack
Remaining portion of Fibre-Filler with milk
from allowance

TOTAL	1,000	38

* Sardine and Cucumber Sandwich

Serves 1

2 large thin slices (2½oz, 70g) wholemeal bread
1·23oz (35g) pot Shippams Sardine Spread with Tomato
1oz (30g) cucumber, sliced
salt and pepper

Spread both slices of the bread with the sardine spread. Full with
the cucumber slices and season with salt and pepper. Cut into four.

1,000 CALORIE MENU		**2**
	Calories	Fibre (g)
Daily allowance: Fibre-Filler (p. 24),		
½ pint (285ml) skimmed milk, an orange		
and an apple or pear	400	20

	Calories	Fibre (g)
Breakfast Half portion of Fibre-Filler with milk from allowance		
Office or work lunch * Ham and Fruit Salad 2 Energen F-Plan Diet Brancrisps, spread with ¼oz (7g) low-fat spread		
An orange from allowance	190	6·5
Evening meal * Cheesy Fish and Tomato Pie 4oz (115g) frozen mixed cauliflower, peas and carrots		
An apple or pear from allowance	410	11
Suppertime snack Remaining portion of Fibre-Filler with milk from allowance		
TOTAL	1,000	37·5

* Ham and Fruit Salad

Serves 1

1oz (30g) sliced boiled lean ham
1 small red-skinned eating apple, additional to allowance
2 teaspoons lemon juice
1oz (30g) black grapes, halved and pips removed
2 sticks celery, chopped
1 tablespoon oil-free French dressing
salt and pepper
a few lettuce leaves

Remove any fat and chop the ham. Core and chop the apple and toss in the lemon juice to prevent browning. Mix the chopped apple with the halved grapes, celery, French dressing and salt and pepper to taste. Arrange the lettuce leaves in the bottom of a plastic carton. Spoon the apple and grape mixture into the carton and top with the chopped ham. Remember to take a fork to work.

* Cheesy Fish and Tomato Pie

Serves 1

6oz (170g) packet frozen cod in mushroom sauce
half medium packet Smash Potato Pieces
1 tomato, sliced
2 tablespoons grated Parmesan cheese

Cook the frozen cod in sauce as directed on the packet. Make up the potato pieces with boiling water as directed (do not add butter). Pipe or spoon the potato around the edges of an individual ovenproof dish. Remove the fish and sauce from the bag and flake the fish into the sauce. Spoon into the potato border. Cover the fish with tomato slices and sprinkle over the grated cheese. Heat through under a hot grill until the cheese is beginning to brown.

1,000 CALORIE MENU 3

	Calories	Fibre (g)
Daily allowance: Fibre-Filler (p. 24), ½ pint (285ml) skimmed milk, an orange and an apple or pear	400	20

Breakfast
Half portion of Fibre-Filler with milk from allowance

	Calories	Fibre (g)

Office or work lunch
2 Energen F-Plan Diet Brancrisps
4oz (115g) Eden Vale Coleslaw in
Vinaigrette
1oz (30g) German salami, sliced
(Pack the ingredients separately to avoid
the crispbreads becoming soggy: at
lunchtime spoon the coleslaw over the
crispbreads and top with sliced salami.)

An apple or pear from allowance	200	7·5

Evening meal
* Jacket Potato with Sausage Topping
3½oz (100g) baked beans in tomato sauce

An orange from allowance	400	12·5

Suppertime snack
Remaining portion of Fibre-Filler with milk
from allowance

TOTAL	1,000	40

* Jacket Potato with Sausage Topping

Serves 1

7oz (200g) potato
2 beef chipolata sausages
1oz (30g) Bicks Corn Relish

Bake the potato following one of the methods on p. 31. Grill the beef chipolatas until well done. Cut the baked potato in half lengthwise and scoop out some of the flesh. Mix with the corn relish and pile back into the potato jacket. Arrange one chipolata sausage on the top of each half jacket potato. Serve with heated baked beans.

1,000 CALORIE MENU **4**

	Calories	Fibre (g)
Daily allowance: Fibre-Filler (p. 24), ½ pint (285ml) skimmed milk, an orange and an apple or pear	400	20

Breakfast
Half portion of Fibre-Filler with milk from allowance

Office or work lunch
1 egg (size 3), hard-boiled and shelled
Salad: a bunch of watercress, a few spring onions or onion rings, 1 stick celery, chopped, 1 carrot cut into small sticks, a few cucumber slices, 1 tomato cut into wedges and 1 tablespoon oil-free French dressing
(Put all the salad vegetables into a plastic container and toss in the French dressing. Seal the container and take to work with the egg wrapped separately.)
2 Energen F-Plan Diet Brancrisps, spread with ½oz (7g) low-fat spread

An apple or pear from allowance	190	6·5

Evening meal
* Spaghetti with Tuna Sauce

2 Energen F-Plan Diet Brancrisps, spread with 1 triangle cheese spread and topped with mustard and cress

An orange from allowance	410	9

	Calories	Fibre (g)
Suppertime snack Remaining portion of Fibre-Filler with milk from allowance		
TOTAL	1,000	35·5

* **Spaghetti with Tuna Sauce**

Serves 1

2oz (55g) wholewheat spaghetti
5oz (140g) canned tomatoes with juice
1 tablespoon finely chopped onion
a pinch dried basil or oregano
3½oz (100g) canned tuna in brine, drained
salt and pepper

Boil the spaghetti in salted water for about 12 minutes or until just tender. Meanwhile, purée the canned tomatoes in a blender or mash well with a fork. Place in a small saucepan with the onion and herbs. Bring to the boil, cover and simmer for 5 minutes. Flake the tuna and add to the sauce in the pan with salt and pepper to taste. Stir well and continue to heat for 3 minutes. Drain the spaghetti and arrange on a serving dish. Spoon the tuna sauce over the spaghetti and serve.

1,000 CALORIE MENU 5

	Calories	Fibre (g)
Daily allowance: Fibre-Filler (p. 24), ½ pint (285ml) skimmed milk, an orange and an apple or pear	400	20

Breakfast
Half portion of Fibre-Filler with milk from
allowance

	Calories	Fibre (g)

Office or work lunch
10·6oz (300g) can Heinz Lentil Soup
2 Energen F-Plan Diet Brancrisps, lightly
spread with Marmite or yeast extract
(Heat the soup and carry to work in a
vacuum flask; wrap the crispbreads.
Remember to take a spoon.)

	Calories	Fibre (g)
An orange from allowance	225	8

Evening meal
* Watercress and Herb Omelet
4oz (115g) fresh or frozen peas

7¾oz (220g) can Boots Shapers Peaches in Low-Calorie Syrup	375	12

Suppertime snack
Remaining portion of Fibre-Filler with milk
from allowance

An apple or pear from allowance

TOTAL	1,000	40

* Watercress and Herb Omelet

Serves 1

3 eggs (size 3)
salt and pepper
1 tablespoon chopped fresh chives and parsley, mixed
¼oz (7g) low-fat spread
1oz (30g) watercress, chopped

Beat the eggs with 1 tablespoon cold water, salt, pepper and fresh herbs. Grease a non-stick omelet pan or small frying pan with the low-fat spread and heat. Pour in the egg mixture and cook until the bottom of the omelet is set and beginning to brown and the top is still slightly runny. Sprinkle the watercress over the centre of the omelet. Fold the omelet and turn out on a warm plate. Serve with peas.

1,000 CALORIE MENU 6

	Calories	Fibre (g)
Daily allowance: 2 tubs Energen F-Plan Crunchy Bran Muesli, ½ pint (285ml) skimmed milk, an orange and an apple or pear	420	20

Breakfast
1 tub Energen F-Plan Crunchy Bran
Muesli with milk from allowance

An orange from allowance

Office or work lunch
* Peanut Butter and Salad Lunch Roll
1 carrot cut into sticks
1 large stick celery, cut into small sticks

An apple or pear from allowance	235	9

Evening meal
6oz (170g) pack Birds Eye Cod in Cheese
Sauce, cooked
4oz (115g) frozen mixed peas, sweetcorn
and peppers
4oz (115g) cabbage, boiled

125g carton Waistline Reduced Calorie Yogurt, black cherry or prune	345	9·5

Suppertime snack
1 tub Energen F-Plan Crunchy Bran
Muesli with milk from allowance

TOTAL	1,000	38·5

* Peanut Butter and Salad Lunch Roll

Serves 1

1 wholemeal lunch roll or bap (2oz, 55g)
½oz (15g) peanut butter
1 tomato, sliced
a few slices cucumber
$\frac{1}{E}$ carton mustard and cress

Split the wholemeal roll in two and spread the bottom half with the peanut butter. Top with the sliced tomato, cucumber and mustard and cress. Replace the top half of the roll. Wrap in cling film.

1,000 CALORIE MENU 7

	Calories	Fibre (g)
Daily allowance: 2 tubs Energen F-Plan Crunchy Bran Muesli, ½ pint (285ml) skimmed milk, an orange and an apple or pear	420	20
Breakfast 1 tub Energen F-Plan Crunchy Bran Muesli with milk from allowance An orange from allowance		
Office or work lunch * Cottage Cheese and Grape Salad 2 Energen F-Plan Diet Brancrisps An average-sized banana (6oz, 170g)	290	7
Evening meal * Cauliflower with Chicken Liver and Mushroom Sauce 3½oz (100g) canned sweetcorn An apple or pear from allowance	290	12·5

	Calories	Fibre (g)
Suppertime snack 1 tub Energen F-Plan Crunchy Bran Muesli with milk from allowance		
TOTAL	1,000	39.5

* Cottage Cheese and Grape Salad

Serves 1

4oz (115g) carton natural cottage cheese
3oz (85g) black grapes, halved and pips removed
1 large stick celery, chopped
salt and pepper
a few lettuce leaves, shredded

Mix the cottage cheese with the halved grapes, chopped celery and seasoning to taste. Line a plastic carton with shredded lettuce and spoon the cottage cheese and grape salad on top. Seal; take a fork to eat it with.

* Cauliflower with Chicken Liver and Mushroom Sauce

Serves 1

4oz (115g) chicken livers, chopped
½ small onion, peeled and chopped
½ clove garlic, crushed (optional)
1 carrot, grated
½ chicken stock cube
salt and pepper
2oz (55g) mushrooms, chopped
6oz (170g) cauliflower, broken into florets

Put the chicken livers, onion, garlic and carrot in a small saucepan. Dissolve the stock cube in 3½fl oz (100ml) boiling water and pour into the pan. Add salt and pepper. Bring to the boil, cover and simmer gently for 20 minutes. Add the mushrooms and simmer for a further 5 minutes. Meanwhile, cook the cauliflower in boiling, salted water until just tender, then drain. Arrange the cauliflower on a serving dish and pour over the chicken liver and mushroom sauce.

1,000 CALORIE MENU   8

	Calories	Fibre (g)
Daily allowance: 2 tubs Energen F-Plan Crunchy Bran Muesli, ½ pint (285ml) skimmed milk, an orange and an apple or pear	420	20
Breakfast 1 tub Energen F-Plan Crunchy Bran Muesli with milk from allowance An orange from allowance		
Office or work lunch * Salmon Pâté and Watercress Lunch Roll An apple or pear from allowance	190	5·5
Evening meal 3½oz (100g) bacon steak, grilled without fat 2 tomatoes, grilled without fat 8oz (225g) canned baked beans with tomato sauce Half medium packet Smash Potato Pieces, made up with water (no butter)	390	23
Suppertime snack 1 tub Energen F-Plan Crunchy Bran Muesli with milk from allowance		
TOTAL	1,000	48·5

* Salmon Pâté and Watercress Lunch Roll

Serves 1

1 wholemeal lunch roll or bap (2oz, 55g)
1·23oz (35g) pot Shippams Salmon Pâté Spread
a small bunch of watercress
1 teaspoon low-calorie salad dressing

Split the roll in half. Spread the salmon spread on the bottom half
of the roll. Cover generously with sprigs of watercress. Spread the
low-calorie salad dressing on the top half of the roll and place on
top of watercress. Wrap in cling film.

1,000 CALORIE MENU   9

	Calories	Fibre (g)
Daily allowance: 2 tubs Energen F-Plan Crunchy Bran Muesli, ½ pint (285ml) skimmed milk, an orange and an apple or pear	420	20
Breakfast 1 tub of Energen F-Plan Crunchy Bran Muesli with milk from allowance		
An orange from allowance		
Office or work lunch 10·6oz (300g) can Heinz Pea & Ham Soup 2 Energen F-Plan Diet Brancrisps, without spread (Heat the soup and pour into a vacuum flask; wrap the crispbreads. Remember to take a spoon.)		
An apple or pear from allowance	245	9

	Calories	Fibre (g)
Evening meal		
* Chicken with Raisin Coleslaw Vinaigrette		
2 Energen F-Plan Diet Brancrisps, spread		
with 1 triangle cheese spread and topped		
with sliced cucumber	335	8·5
Suppertime snack		
1 tub Energen F-Plan Crunchy Bran		
Muesli with milk from allowance		

TOTAL	1,000	37·5

* Chicken with Raisin Coleslaw Vinaigrette

Serves 1

1 chicken leg joint (8oz. 225g raw weight)
3oz (85g) white cabbage, shredded
1 medium carrot, grated
1 large stick celery, finely chopped
½oz (15g) raisins
2 tablespoons oil-free French dressing

Grill the chicken joint without added fat, turning over until cooked through. To make the coleslaw, mix the cabbage, carrot, celery, raisins and French dressing until well blended. Remove the skin from the grilled chicken joint and serve with the coleslaw.

1,000 CALORIE MENU 10

	Calories	Fibre (g)
Daily allowance: 2 tubs Energen F-Plan		
Crunchy Bran Muesli, ½ pint (285ml)		
skimmed milk, an orange and an apple or		
pear	420	20

	Calories	Fibre (g)

Breakfast
1 tub Energen F-Plan Crunchy Bran
Muesli with milk from allowance

Office or work lunch
2 pork chipolata sausages, well grilled and
then left to go cold
8oz (226g) carton Eden Vale Coleslaw with
Low Calorie Dressing
(Wrap the sausages separately and take to
work with the salad. Remember to take a
fork.)

An apple or pear from allowance	245	4·5

Evening meal
* Baked Jacket Potato with Cheesy Filling
4oz (115g) canned baked beans with
tomato sauce

An orange from allowance	335	13·5

Suppertime snack
1 tub Energen F-Plan Crunch Bran
Muesli with milk from allowance

TOTAL	1,000	38

* **Baked Jacket Potato with Cheesy Filling**

Serves 1

7oz (200g) potato
2oz (55g) cottage cheese (natural or with chives or with onion
   and peppers)
½oz (15g) Bicks Corn Relish
salt and pepper
2 level teaspoons grated Parmesan cheese

Bake the potato following one of the methods on p. 31. Cut the potato in half lengthwise and scoop out some of the flesh. Add the cottage cheese, corn relish and salt and pepper to taste to the potato flesh and mash together. Pile the cheese and potato mixture back into the potato jacket. Sprinkle 1 teaspoon Parmesan cheese over the top of each half of jacket potato and then heat through under the grill until the cheese begins to brown. Serve hot.

1,250 CALORIE MENU   1

	Calories	Fibre (g)
Daily allowance: Fibre-Filler (p. 24), ½ pint (285ml) skimmed milk, an orange and an apple or pear	400	20

Breakfast
Half portion of Fibre-Filler with milk from allowance

An orange from allowance

Office or work lunch
* Devilled Egg Sandwich

125g carton Waistline Reduced Calorie Yogurt, black cherry, strawberry or prune

An apple or pear from allowance	345	7·5

Evening meal
* Thatched Cod and Broccoli
4oz (115g) fresh or frozen broad beans, boiled

3½oz (100g) green grapes	455	14

	Calories	Fibre (g)
Suppertime snack		
Remaining portion of Fibre-Filler with milk from allowance		
1 Energen F-Plan Diet Brancrisp, spread with 2 level tablespoons Waistline Country Vegetable Spread	50	1·5
TOTAL	1,250	43

* Devilled Egg Sandwich

Serves 1

1 tablespoon low-calorie salad dressing
½ teaspoon Worcestershire sauce
1 medium carrot, grated
2 large thin slices (2½oz, 70g) wholemeal bread
1 egg (size 3), hard-boiled and sliced
¼ carton mustard and cress

Mix the low-calorie salad dressing with the Worcestershire sauce and grated carrot. Divide between the two slices of bread and spread over the bread. Arrange the egg slices and mustard and cress over one slice of bread and cover with the second slice. Cut into four; wrap in cling film for carrying.

* Thatched Cod and Broccoli

Serves 1

6oz (170g) frozen broccoli
6oz (170g) pack frozen cod in cheese or butter sauce
salt and pepper
1oz (30g) fresh wholemeal breadcrumbs
½oz (15g) grated Cheddar cheese

Cook the broccoli and the cod according to pack instructions. Drain the broccoli and season with salt and pepper. Place in a shallow ovenproof dish. Put the cod and sauce on top of the broccoli. Mix the breadcrumbs with the grated cheese and sprinkle on top. Heat under the grill until the topping is crisp and golden brown.

1,250 CALORIE MENU   2

	Calories	Fibre (g)
Daily allowance: Fibre-Filler (p. 24), ½ pint (285 ml) skimmed milk, an orange and an apple or pear	400	20
Breakfast Half portion of Fibre-Filler with milk from allowance		
1 large thin slice wholemeal bread, toasted and spread with ¼oz (7g) low-fat spread and 1 level teaspoon marmalade or honey	115	3
Office or work lunch 1 Wimpy hamburger with bun		
An orange from allowance	325	1·5
Evening meal 1 pork chop (7oz, 200g raw weight), well grilled and with fat cut off after grilling, served with 1 ring of pineapple from a can of pineapple in natural juice, heated through under grill 4oz (115g) mushrooms, poached in a little stock *or* 7½oz (215g) canned button mushrooms in brine, heated through and drained 4oz (115g) frozen peas, boiled		
An apple or pear from allowance	410	12·5

	Calories	Fibre (g)
Suppertime snack Remaining portion of Fibre-Filler with milk from allowance		
TOTAL	1,250	37

1,250 CALORIE MENU 3

	Calories	Fibre (g)
Daily allowance: Fibre-Filler (p. 24), ½ pint (285ml) skimmed milk, an orange and an apple or pear	400	20
Breakfast Half portion Fibre-Filler with milk from allowance		
A large banana (7½oz. 215g)	95	4·5
Office or work lunch * Corned Beef and Corn Relish Lunch Roll 2oz (55g) carrot, cut into sticks		
An orange from allowance	310	8
Evening meal * Grilled Spiced Chicken with Stir-Fry Vegetables		
An apple or pear from allowance	445	6·5
Suppertime snack Remaining portion of Fibre-Filler with milk from allowance		
TOTAL	1,250	39

* Corned Beef and Corn Relish Lunch Roll

Serves 1

1 wholemeal lunch roll or bap (2oz, 55g)
¼oz (7g) low-fat spread
2oz (55g) corned beef, sliced
1oz (30g) Bicks Corn Relish
a few sprigs of watercress

Split the wholemeal roll in two and spread the cut surfaces lightly with low-fat spread. Arrange the sliced corned beef on the bottom half of the roll and top with corn relish and sprigs of watercress. Replace the top half of the roll. Wrap in cling film.

* Grilled Spiced Chicken with Stir-Fry Vegetables

Serves 1

1 chicken leg joint (8oz, 225g raw weight)
1oz (30g) Branston Spicy Sauce
10oz (285g) pack Birds Eye Continental Stir-Fry Vegetables

Remove the skin from the chicken leg joint and brush all over with the sauce. Cook on a piece of foil under the grill, turning once or twice, until cooked through. Meanwhile cook the vegetables according to the pack instructions. Serve with the grilled chicken.

1,250 CALORIE MENU   4

	Calories	Fibre (g)
Daily allowance: Fibre-Filler (p. 24), ½ pint (285ml) skimmed milk, an orange and an apple or pear	400	20

Breakfast
Half portion of Fibre-Filler with milk from
allowance
1 egg (size 3), poached and served on 1
large thin slice (1¼oz, 35g) wholemeal

	Calories	Fibre (g)
bread, toasted and spread with 1 tablespoon tomato ketchup	170	3

Office or work lunch
15·3oz (435g) can Heinz Vegetable & Lentil Big Soup
2 Energen F-Plan Diet Brancrisps, lightly spread with Marmite or yeast extract
(Heat the soup and carry to work in a vacuum flask; wrap the crispbreads.)

	Calories	Fibre (g)
An apple or pear from allowance	255	11

Evening meal
5oz (140g) lamb loin chop, well grilled
4oz (115g) Brussels sprouts, boiled
4oz (115g) carrots, boiled

	Calories	Fibre (g)
4oz (115g) canned pineapple slices in natural juice	415	7·5

Suppertime snack
Remaining portion Fibre-Filler with milk from allowance

	Calories	Fibre (g)
2oz (55g) carrot sticks	10	1·5
TOTAL	**1,250**	**43**

1,250 CALORIE MENU   5

	Calories	Fibre (g)
Daily allowance: Fibre-Filler (p.24), ½ pint (285ml) skimmed milk, an orange and an apple or pear	400	20

	Calories	Fibre (g)

Breakfast
Half portion Fibre-Filler with milk from
allowance

1 large thin slice (1½oz, 35g) wholemeal
bread, toasted and spread with ¼oz (7g)
low-fat spread and 1 level teaspoon
marmalade or honey · · · · · · · · · 115 · · · 3

Office or work lunch
2oz (55g) boiled lean ham with any fat
trimmed off
2 Energen F-Plan Diet Brancrisps, spread
with ¼oz (7g) low-fat spread mixed with a
little made mustard
8oz (226g) carton Eden Vale Coleslaw in
Vinaigrette
(Pack the ham slices and crispbreads
separately and leave the coleslaw in its
carton. Place the ham slices on the
crispbreads to eat; pack a fork for the salad.)
An apple or pear from allowance · · · · 195 · · · 6·5

Evening meal
* Baked Jacket Potato with Egg and
Tomato Filling
4oz (115g) canned baked beans with tomato
sauce
2oz (55g) vanilla ice-cream served with
the orange from allowance, segmented · · 460 · · · 14

Suppertime snack
Remaining portion Fibre-Filler with milk
from allowance
An average-sized banana (6oz, 170g) · · · 80 · · · 3·5

| TOTAL | 1,250 | 47 |

* Baked Jacket Potato with Egg and Tomato Filling

Serves 1

7oz (200g) potato
1 egg (size 3)
2 tablespoons skimmed milk from allowance
¼oz (7g) low-fat spread
salt and pepper
1 medium tomato or 1 canned tomato, chopped

Bake the potato in the oven at 200°C (400°F, gas 6) for 45 minutes or until soft when pinched. Scramble the egg with the skimmed milk, low-fat spread and salt and pepper in a small saucepan. Stir in the chopped tomato and heat through. Cut the potato in half lengthwise and scoop out some of the flesh. Mash the potato flesh and mix with the scrambled egg and tomato. Pile back into the potato jacket and serve.

1,250 CALORIE MENU   6

This menu is suitable for vegetarians

	Calories	Fibre (g)
Daily allowance: 2 tubs Energen F-Plan Crunchy Bran Muesli, ½ pint (285 ml) skimmed milk, an orange and an apple or pear	420	20

Breakfast
1 tub Energen F-Plan Crunchy Bran Muesli with milk from allowance

An orange from allowance

Office or work lunch
* Waldorf Salad

1 Quaker Harvest Crunch Bar, almond or peanut	340	9

	Calories	Fibre (g)
Evening meal		
* One Pan Pasta Dish	420	6
Suppertime snack		
1 tub Energen F-Plan Crunchy Bran		
Muesli with milk from allowance		
An apple or pear from allowance		
TOTAL	1,250	35

* **Waldorf Salad**

Serves 1

3oz (85g) red cabbage, shredded
1 large stick celery, chopped
1 small (about 4oz, 115g) green eating apple, additional to
    allowance, cored and chopped
2 teaspoons lemon juice
1oz (30g) walnuts, shelled, roughly chopped
2 tablespoons low-calorie salad dressing

Mix the red cabbage and celery together. Toss the apple in the
lemon juice and then add to the cabbage and celery with the
walnuts and the salad dressing. Mix well until the salad ingredients
are thoroughly blended. Pack in a plastic carton and seal with a
lid. Pack a fork.

* **One Pan Pasta Dish**

Serves 1

1oz (30g) wholewheat spaghetti or macaroni
½oz (15g) low-fat spread
1 small onion, peeled and chopped
2oz (55g) mushrooms, sliced
1 medium tomato, chopped
2 eggs (size 3)

4 tablespoons skimmed milk, additional to allowance
salt and pepper
½oz (15g) grated mature Cheddar cheese

Boil the spaghetti or macaroni in salted water for about 12
minutes or until just tender. Heat the low-fat spread in a pan, add
the onion and cook gently until soft. Add the mushrooms and
tomato and cook for a further 3–4 minutes. Add the drained cooked
spaghetti or macaroni and heat through. Beat the eggs with the
milk and salt and pepper. Pour over the pasta mixture and cook
over a low heat, stirring continuously, until sauce begins to thick-
en. Do not allow to boil. Remove from heat and serve immediately,
sprinkled with the grated cheese.

1,250 CALORIE MENU 7

This menu is suitable for vegetarians

	Calories	Fibre (g)
Daily allowance: 2 tubs Energen F-Plan Crunchy Bran Muesli, ½ pint (285ml) skimmed milk, an orange and an apple or pear	420	20
Breakfast 1 tub Energen F-Plan Crunchy Bran Muesli with milk from allowance 1 Energen F-Plan Diet Brancrisp, spread with 1 level teaspoon honey	35	1
Office or work lunch 1 sachet Batchelors Slim-a-Soup, beef and tomato or chicken and golden vegetable Cheese, tomato and cucumber sandwich: 2 large thin slices (2½oz, 70g) wholemeal bread, spread with 1 triangle cheese spread and filled with 1 medium tomato, sliced and a few slices of cucumber An apple or pear from allowance	240	7

	Calories	Fibre (g)

Evening meal
* Vegetable and Cheese Pie
2 Energen F-Plan Diet Brancrisps, spread
with Marmite or yeast extract

An orange from allowance	480	15·5

Suppertime snack
1 tub Energen F-Plan Crunchy Bran
Muesli with milk from allowance 125g
carton Waistline Reduced Calorie yogurt,

any fruit flavour	75	0

TOTAL	1,250	43·5

* Vegetable and Cheese Pie

Serves 1

½oz (15g) low-fat spread
½oz (15g) wholemeal flour
¼ pint (140ml) skimmed milk, additional to allowance
salt and pepper
¼ teaspoon made mustard
1oz (30g) mature Cheddar cheese, grated
7½oz (215g) canned butter beans
4oz (115g) frozen mixed vegetables

Put the low-fat spread, flour and milk into a small saucepan and heat gently, whisking continuously, until the mixture boils and thickens. Season to taste with salt and pepper and stir in the mustard and half the grated cheese. Remove from the heat. Heat the can of butter beans and drain. Cook the frozen mixed vegetables according to instructions and drain. Mix the butter beans and mixed vegetables with the cheese sauce and turn into a small ovenproof dish. Sprinkle over the remaining grated cheese and heat under the grill until the cheese is melted and beginning to brown.

1,250 CALORIE MENU 8

	Calories	Fibre (g)
Daily allowance: 2 tubs Energen F-Plan Crunchy Bran Muesli, ½ pint (285ml) skimmed milk, an orange and an apple or pear	420	20

Breakfast
Both tubs Energen F-Plan Crunchy Bran Muesli with milk from allowance

Office or work lunch
1 McCain Deep 'n' Delicious Ham & Mushroom Pizza, cooked according to instructions, cooled, cut into four pieces and wrapped
Mixed salad: a few lettuce leaves, shredded, 1 tomato, cut into wedges, a few cucumber slices, a few spring onions, chopped
(Pack in a plastic carton.)

An apple or pear from allowance	205	3

Evening meal
* Bean and Frankfurter Supper

2oz (55g) vanilla ice-cream, served with an orange from allowance, cut into segments	510	20

Suppertime snack
1 large thin slice (1¼oz, 35g) wholemeal bread, toasted and spread with 1 triangle cheese spread

cheese spread	115	3

TOTAL	1,250	46

* Bean and Frankfurter Supper

Serves 1

8oz (225g) canned baked beans with tomato sauce
1 teaspoon Worcestershire sauce
½ teaspoon made mustard
1 tablespoon finely chopped onion
1 canned tomato, chopped
2 tablespoons tomato juice from canned tomatoes
2oz (55g) frankfurter, sliced
1 large thin slice (1¼oz, 35g) wholemeal bread

Mix all the ingredients together in a saucepan. Heat to simmering point, cover and cook over a gentle heat for 15 minutes. Meanwhile, toast the slice of bread. Pile the bean and frankfurter mixture on the toast.

1,250 CALORIE MENU   9

	Calories	Fibre (g)
Daily allowance: 2 tubs Energen F-Plan Crunchy Bran Muesli, ½ pint (285ml) skimmed milk, an orange and an apple or pear	420	20
Breakfast 1 tub Energen F-Plan Crunchy Bran Muesli with milk from allowance 1 egg (size 3), poached and served on 1 large thin slice (1¼oz, 35g) wholemeal bread, toasted and spread with ⅛oz (7g) low-fat spread	180	3
Office or work lunch Cottage cheese and date sandwich: 2 large thin slices (2½oz, 70g) wholemeal bread filled with 2oz (55g) natural cottage cheese mixed with 1oz (30g) chopped stoned dates		
An apple or pear from allowance	275	8·5

	Calories	Fibre (g)
Evening meal		
* Tuna and Sweetcorn in Seafood Sauce with Cauliflower		
8oz (226g) can Koo Peach Slices in Apple Juice		
2 tablespoons low-fat natural yogurt	375	9
Suppertime snack		
1 tub Energen F-Plan Crunchy Bran Muesli with milk from allowance		
An orange from allowance		
TOTAL	1,250	40·5

* Tuna and Sweetcorn in Seafood Sauce with Cauliflower

Serves 1

half packet Knorr Seafood Sauce Mix
¼ pint (140ml) skimmed milk, additional to allowance
3½oz (100g) canned tuna in brine, drained and flaked
2oz (55g) canned sweetcorn kernels
6oz (170g) cauliflower, broken into florets

Put the sauce mix into a small saucepan and add a little of the milk. Blend to a smooth cream, then stir in the remaining milk. Bring slowly to the boil, stirring continuously. Lower the heat, continue to stir and simmer for 3 minutes. Add the flaked tuna and sweetcorn to the sauce and heat through. Cook the cauliflower in boiling salted water until just tender, about 10 minutes. Drain well and arrange on a serving dish. Pour the sauce over the cauliflower and serve immediately.

1,250 CALORIE MENU   10

	Calories	Fibre (g)
Daily allowance: 2 tubs Energen F-Plan Crunchy Bran Muesli, ½ pint (285ml) skimmed milk, an orange and an apple or pear	420	20

Breakfast
2 tubs Energen F-Plan Crunchy Bran
Muesli with milk from allowance

Office or work lunch
* Kidney Beans, Mushroom, Sweetcorn and
Cheese Salad

An orange from allowance	215	11·5

Evening meal
* Liver and Bacon in a Pot
Half a medium packet Smash Potato Pieces
made up with boiling water as instructed
(no butter) *or* 5oz (140g) potatoes, boiled
and mashed with a little skimmed milk from

allowance (no butter)	455	8

Suppertime snack
1 large thin slice (1½oz, 35g) wholemeal
bread, toasted, topped with 1oz (30g) Edam
cheese, grated and heated under the grill

until the cheese has melted	160	3

TOTAL	1,250	42·5

* Kidney Beans, Mushroom, Sweetcorn and Cheese Salad

Serves 1

3oz (85g) canned red kidney beans, drained
2oz (55g) button mushrooms, sliced
2oz (55g) canned sweetcorn kernels
1oz (30g) Edam cheese, diced
2 tablespoons oil-free French dressing

Mix all the ingredients together well. Pack in a plastic carton. Remember to pack a fork.

* Liver and Bacon in a Pot

Serves 1

¼oz (7g) low-fat spread
1 rasher streaky bacon, rind removed and chopped
1 medium carrot, sliced
1 small onion, peeled and sliced
4oz (115g) lamb's liver, thinly sliced
8oz (225g) canned tomatoes
a pinch of dried thyme
salt and pepper

Melt the low-fat spread in a saucepan and add the bacon, carrot and onion. Cover and cook gently for 5 minutes, shaking the pan from time to time. Turn into a small ovenproof casserole and lay the liver slices on top. Chop the tomatoes in their juice and spoon over the liver. Sprinkle over the thyme and season well with salt and pepper. Cover and cook in a slow oven at 150°C (300°F, gas 2) for 1 hour. Serve with mashed potato.

SNACK EATER'S
F-PLAN

Many women who are at home most of the day tend to eat frequent snacks. If this pattern of eating is your norm, these menus of five small snack meals a day will provide your easiest F-Plan method. And there is no harm – you may even lose weight slightly faster – in eating little and often, as long as your total food and fibre intake is correct for the day.

The menus all follow the basic F-Plan rules (p. 23). The snack meals are all simple and quick to prepare, both to reduce to a minimum the time spent in the kitchen and because snack eaters and nibblers tend to prefer more or less instant foods.

As with the 'Simply F-Plan' menus these snack eater's menus are divided into two sections – menus providing 1,000 calories and menus providing 1,250 calories daily – to enable you to choose menus which will result in the best weight loss for you.

SPECIAL DIET RULES

1. Decide which daily calorie total will give you the best weight loss. For guidance on the most suitable daily calorie allowance for you, see p. 26.

2. Plan ahead and select at least two or three menus, preferably one week's menus, at a time to enable you to shop for the foods you need.

3. Make sure that you eat a variety of foods by selecting several different menus each week, to be sure that you are getting all the nutrients you need for good health.

4. The five snack meals from your daily menu can be eaten in any order and at any time of day you wish. However, it is inadvisable to swap one snack meal from one menu with a meal from another menu, since this will usually alter the amount of calories and fibre which have been carefully counted for each full day's menu.

5. Drinks can be taken at any time during the day and in any

quantity provided that you stick to unsugared tea and coffee, either black or with skimmed milk from the daily allowance (reserve some to eat with the Fibre-Filler), low-calorie-labelled bottled and canned drinks, and water. If you feel the need to have an alcoholic drink occasionally then see the advice given on p. 285 and select a drink from the chart on p. 285.

1,000 CALORIE MENU   1

	Calories	Fibre (g)
Daily allowance: Fibre-Filler (p. 24), ½ pint (285 ml) skimmed milk, an orange and an apple or pear	400	20
Meal 1 Half portion of Fibre-Filler with milk from allowance		
Meal 2 1 egg (size 3), poached and served on 1 large thin slice (1¼oz, 35g) wholemeal bread, toasted and spead with ¼oz (7g) low-fat spread	180	3
Meal 3 10·6oz (300g) can Heinz Lentil Soup, 1 Energen F-Plan Diet Branscrisp, spread with 2 level tablespoons Waistline Low Calorie Vegetable Spread, any variety		
An apple or pear from allowance	230	7
Meal 4 2 frozen cod fish cakes, grilled without fat, 1 medium tomato, halved and grilled without fat		

	Calories	Fibre (g)
4oz (115g) frozen peas, boiled	190	12

Meal 5
Remaining portion of Fibre-Filler with milk
from allowance

An orange from allowance

TOTAL	1,000	42

1,000 CALORIE MENU   2

	Calories	Fibre (g)
Daily allowance: Fibre-Filler (p. 24), $\frac{1}{2}$ pint (285ml) skimmed milk, an orange and an apple or pear	400	20

Meal 1
Half portion of Fibre-Filler with milk from
allowance

An orange from allowance

Meal 2
Cottage cheese and cumcumber sandwich:
2 large thin slices (2½oz, 70g) wholemeal
bread filled with 2oz (55g) cottage cheese
(natural, with chives, with onions and
peppers, or with pineapple), salt and pepper
to taste and 1oz (30g) sliced cucumber   210   6

Meal 3
150g carton low-fat natural yogurt mixed
with an average-sized banana (6oz, 170g),
sliced and 2 walnut halves, chopped   190   4

	Calories	Fibre (g)
Meal 4		
1 frozen beefburger, well grilled		
1 medium tomato, grilled without fat		
4oz (115g) baked beans in tomato sauce	200	9

Meal 5
Remaining portion of Fibre-Filler with milk from allowance

An apple or pear from allowance

TOTAL	1,000	39

1,000 CALORIE MENU 3

	Calories	Fibre (g)
Daily allowance: Fibre-Filler (p. 24), ½ pint (285 ml) skimmed milk, an orange and an apple or pear	400	20

Meal 1
Half portion of Fibre-Filler with milk from allowance

An orange from allowance

Meal 2		
2 Energen F-Plan Diet Brancrisps, each topped with 1 medium tomato, sliced, 1 sardine canned in tomato sauce and 1 small gherkin, chopped		
An apple or pear from allowance	165	4

	Calories	Fibre (g)
Meal 3 7½oz (215g) canned prunes in syrup with 1 tablespoon natural yogurt	245	9
Meal 4 1 frozen cod steak, covered with 1 table spoon chopped onion, 4oz (115g) canned tomatoes, salt and pepper to taste and a pinch of mixed herbs, covered and baked at 180°C (350°F, gas 4) for 25 minutes		
4oz (115g) frozen mixed vegetables, boiled	155	6·5
Meal 5 Remaining portion of Fibre-Filler with milk from allowance		
1 Energen F-Plan Diet Brancrisp, spread with Marmite or yeast extract and topped with 2oz (55g) grated carrot	35	2·5
TOTAL	1,000	42

1,000 CALORIE MENU   4

	Calories	Fibre (g)
Daily allowance: Fibre-Filler (p. 24), ½ pint (285 ml) skimmed milk, an orange and an apple or pear	400	20
Meal 1 Half portion of Fibre-Filler with milk from allowance		

	Calories	Fibre (g)
1 Energen F-Plan Diet Brancrisp, spread with half a 1¼oz (35g) pot Princes Salmon Spread and topped with a little mustard and cress	40	1

Meal 2

	Calories	Fibre (g)
2 rashers streaky bacon, well grilled, served with 4oz (115g) baked beans in tomato sauce and 1 tomato, halved	180	9

Meal 3

	Calories	Fibre (g)
4oz (115g) carton cottage cheese (natural, with chives, with onions and peppers or with pineapple) Salad: a few lettuce leaves, a 1 inch (2·5cm) piece of cucumber, sliced, 1 medium tomato, sliced, 2 spring onions, chopped *or* ½oz (15g) onion rings, 1oz (30g) green or red pepper, chopped, 1 stick celery, chopped and 1 tablespoon oil-free French dressing, 1 Energen Brancrisp crispbread	165	4

Meal 4

	Calories	Fibre (g)
1 small packet (25g) potato crisps, any flavour 2 large sticks celery, cut into small sticks		
125g carton Waistline Reduced Calorie Yogurt, any fruit flavour	215	5

Meal 5
Remaining portion of Fibre-Filler with milk from allowance

	Calories	Fibre (g)
An orange and an apple or pear from allowance		
TOTAL	1,000	39

1,000 CALORIE MENU 5

	Calories	Fibre (g)
Daily allowance: Fibre-Filler (p. 24), ½ pint (285ml) skimmed milk, an orange and an apple or pear	400	20

Meal 1
Half portion of Fibre-Filler with milk from allowance

An orange from allowance

Meal 2
Ham and pickle sandwich: 2 large thin slices (2½oz, 70g) wholemeal bread spread with 1oz (30g) sweet pickle and filled with 1oz (30g) sliced ham and a few cucumber slices

An apple or pear from allowance   235   6·5

Meal 3
Mexican omelet: beat 2 eggs (size 3), with 2 tablespoons water and salt and pepper. Grease a small non-stick omelet pan with a little low-fat spread. Heat the pan, add the egg mixture and cook until the egg is just set. Spoon 2oz (55g) canned sweetcorn with

	Calories	Fibre (g)
peppers into the centre. Fold the omelet in half and serve with a bunch of watercress	220	4

Meal 4
8oz (225g) canned pear halves in apple juice
1 tablespoon low-fat natural yogurt

	Calories	Fibre (g)
	115	4

Meal 5
Remaining portion of Fibre-Filler with milk from allowance

1 large stick celery filled with 1oz (30g) cottage cheese

	Calories	Fibre (g)
	30	1

TOTAL	1,000	35·5

1,000 CALORIE MENU   6

	Calories	Fibre (g)
Daily allowance: Fibre-Filler (p. 24), ½ pint (285ml) skimmed milk, an orange and an apple or pear	400	20

Meal 1
Half portion of Fibre-Filler with milk from allowance

1 average-sized banana (6oz, 170g)

	Calories	Fibre (g)
	80	3·5

Meal 2
1 sachet Batchelors Slim-A-Soup, golden vegetable, made up with boiling water
2 Energen F-Plan Diet Brancrisps, each spread with 1 level tablespoon Waistline Low Calorie Vegetable Spread, any variety, and topped with 2oz (55g) grated carrot

	Calories	Fibre (g)
	125	4

	Calories	Fibre (g)

Meal 3
150g carton low-fat fruit-flavoured yogurt
mixed with 2 level tablespoons Toasted Bran

| An orange from allowance | 145 | 2 |

Meal 4
6oz (170g) pack frozen cod in mushroom
sauce, cooked

| 4oz (115g) frozen peas, boiled | 250 | 9 |

Meal 5
Remaining portion of Fibre-Filler with milk
from allowance

An apple or pear from allowance

| TOTAL | 1,000 | 38·5 |

1,000 CALORIE MENU   7

	Calories	Fibre (g)

Daily allowance: Fibre-Filler (p. 24),
½ pint (285ml) skimmed milk, an orange

| and an apple or pear | 400 | 20 |

Meal 1
Half portion of Fibre-Filler served with 125g
carton Waistline Reduced Calorie Yogurt,

| prune flavour | 75 | 0 |

Meal 2
1 egg (size 3), boiled and served with 1 large
thin slice (1¼oz, 35g) wholemeal bread
spread with ¼oz (7g) low-fat spread

| An orange from allowance | 180 | 3 |

	Calories	Fibre (g)

Meal 3
4oz (115g) cottage cheese, natural, mixed
with an apple or pear from allowance,
cored and chopped and 1oz (30g) sultanas
or raisins, served on a bed of lettuce
leaves and garnished with 2oz (55g) carrot,
grated

200   4

Meal 4
Bean and tomato hot-pot: heat 4oz (115g)
canned baked beans in tomato sauce with
8oz (225 g) canned tomatoes, a generous
dash of Worcestershire sauce and salt and
pepper to taste. Grill 1 rasher streaky bacon
until crisp. Pour the bean and tomato
hot-pot into a soup bowl and crumble the
bacon over the top

145   10

Meal 5
Remaining portion of Fibre-Filler with milk
from allowance

TOTAL	1,000	37

1,000 CALORIE MENU   8

	Calories	Fibre (g)

Daily allowance: Fibre-Filler (p. 24),
½ pint (285ml) skimmed milk, an orange
and an apple or pear

400   20

Meal 1
Half portion of Fibre-Filler with milk from
allowance

	Calories	Fibre (g)
Meal 2 1 Prewett's Fruit & Bran Bar		
An average-sized banana (6oz, 170g)	165	8·5
Meal 3 1 packet Birds Eye Braised Kidneys in Gravy 4oz (115g) cabbage, boiled		
An orange from allowance	215	3
Meal 4 10·6oz (300g) can Heinz Lentil Soup		
An apple or pear from allowance	180	6
Meal 5 Remaining portion of Fibre-Filler with milk from allowance		
1 Energen F-Plan Diet Brancrisp, spread with half a 1½oz, (35g) pot Princes Salmon Spread and topped with a little mustard and cress	40	1
TOTAL	1,000	38·5

1,000 CALORIE MENU   9

	Calories	Fibre (g)
Daily allowance: Fibre-Filler (p. 24), ½ pint (285ml) skimmed milk, an orange and an apple or pear	400	20
Meal 1 Half portion of Fibre-Filler with milk from allowance		
An orange from allowance		

	Calories	Fibre (g)
Meal 2 8oz (225g) canned baked beans in tomato sauce served on 1 large thin slice (1¼oz, 35g) wholemeal bread, toasted	235	19·5
Meal 3 2oz (55g) peeled prawns, served with a few lettuce leaves, small bunch watercress, 1 inch (2·5cm) cucumber, sliced, 1 medium tomato, sliced, 1 large stick celery, chopped, 1oz (30g) green pepper, sliced, and 1 tablespoon oil-free French dressing		
An apple or pear from allowance	95	4
Meal 4 7½oz (220g) Boots Shapers Apricots in Low-Calorie Syrup 2oz (55g) vanilla ice-cream 2 level tablespoons Toasted Bran (Top the canned apricots with the ice-cream and sprinkle with the Toasted Bran.)	150	5
Meal 5 Remaining portion of Fibre-Filler with milk from allowance		
150g carton low-fat fruit-flavoured yogurt	120	0
TOTAL	1,000	48·5

1,000 CALORIE MENU   10

	Calories	Fibre (g)
Daily allowance: Fibre-Filler (p. 24), ½ pint (285ml) skimmed milk, an orange and an apple or pear	400	20

	Calories	Fibre (g)

Meal 1
Half portion of Fibre-Filler with milk from
allowance

Meal 2
1 large thin slice (1½oz, 35g) wholemeal
bread, toasted, topped with 1 medium
tomato, sliced, sprinkled with a pinch
dried thyme and salt and pepper and
covered with 1oz (30g) mature Cheddar
cheese, grated. Heat through under grill
until the cheese is melted and beginning to
brown

An apple or pear from allowance	200	4

Meal 3
8oz (226g) carton Eden Vale Coleslaw in
Vinaigrette
2oz (55g) boiled lean ham
1oz (30g) pickled beetroot

1 Energen F-Plan Diet Brancrisp	200	8

Meal 4
2oz (55g) vanilla ice-cream
An orange from allowance, segmented

1 Prewett's Banana Dessert Bar	170	2·5

Meal 5
Remaining portion of Fibre-Filler with milk
from allowance

1 Energen F-Plan Diet Brancrisp, spread
with Marmite or yeast extract and topped
with 1 chopped pickled onion or 1oz (30g)

chopped green pepper	30	1·5
TOTAL	**1.000**	**36**

1,250 CALORIE MENU   1

	Calories	Fibre (g)
Daily allowance: Fibre-Filler (p. 24), ½ pint (285ml) skimmed milk, an orange and an apple or pear	400	20

Meal 1
Half portion of Fibre-Filler with milk from allowance

1 large thin slice (1¼oz, 35g) wholemeal bread, spread with ¼oz (7g) low-fat spread and 1 level teaspoon honey or marmalade	115	3

Meal 2
2 frozen fish fingers, grilled without fat
4oz (115g) canned tomatoes, heated
4oz (115g) button mushrooms poached in stock *or* 7½oz (215g) canned button mushrooms in brine, heated and drained   125   4

Meal 3
150g carton low-fat natural yogurt with an apple or pear from allowance, cored and chopped

1oz (30g) raisins or sultanas	150	2

Meal 4
8oz (225g) frozen shepherd's pie
4oz (115g) frozen peas, boiled
4oz (115g) carrots, boiled

An orange from allowance   355   13

	Calories	Fibre (g)
Meal 5 Remaining portion of Fibre-Filler with milk from allowance		
2 Energen F-Plan Diet Brancrisps, spread with 1·23oz (35g) Shippams Beef & Tomato Country Pot Paste and topped with 1 medium tomato, sliced	105	3
TOTAL	1,250	45

1,250 CALORIE MENU 2

	Calories	Fibre (g)
Daily allowance: Fibre-Filler (p. 24), ½ pint (285ml) skimmed milk, an orange and an apple or pear	400	20
Meal 1 Half portion of Fibre-Filler with milk from allowance		
An average-sized banana (6oz, 170g)	80	3·5
Meal 2 2 large thin slices (2½oz, 70g) wholemeal bread, toasted and spread with 2oz (55g) cottage cheese mixed with 1oz (30g) corn relish and topped with 2 medium tomatoes, sliced and heated through under the grill		
An apple or pear from allowance	255	9
Meal 3 Remaining portion of Fibre-Filler with milk from allowance		
An orange from allowance		

	Calories	Fibre (g)
Meal 4		
4oz (115g) lamb's liver, sliced, brushed with 1 teaspoon oil and grilled		
1 rasher streaky bacon, well grilled		
1 medium tomato, halved and grilled without fat		
4oz (115g) cabbage, boiled	315	4
Meal 5		
10·6oz (300g) can Heinz Lentil Soup		
1 Energen F-Plan Diet Brancrisp	200	7
TOTAL	1,250	43·5

1,250 CALORIE MENU   3

	Calories	Fibre (g)
Daily allowance: Fibre-Filler (p. 24), ½ pint (285ml) skimmed milk, an orange and an apple or pear	400	20
Meal 1		
Half portion of Fibre-Filler with milk from allowance		
2 Energen F-Plan Diet Brancrisps, spread with ¼oz (7g) low-fat spread and 2 level teaspoons honey or marmalade	100	2
Meal 2		
Banana, honey and raisin sandwich: 2 large thin slices (2½oz, 70g) wholemeal bread, filled with 6oz (170g) banana, mashed with 2 level teaspoons honey and mixed with 1oz (30g) raisins		
An apple or pear from allowance	330	11·5

	Calories	Fibre (g)
Meal 3		
1 McCain Deep 'n' Delicious Ham &		
Mushroom Pizza		
small bunch of watercress		
1 medium tomato	200	3·5
Meal 4		
7½oz (215g) canned spaghetti in tomato		
sauce topped with ½oz (15g) grated Edam		
cheese and heated under grill until cheese		
melts	190	2
Meal 5		
Remaining portion of Fibre-Filler with milk		
from allowance		
An orange from allowance, segmented and		
mixed with 3 level tablespoons low-fat		
natural yogurt	30	0

TOTAL	1,250	39

1,250 CALORIE MENU 4

	Calories	Fibre (g)
Daily allowance: Fibre-Filler (p. 24),		
½ pint (285ml) skimmed milk, an orange		
and an apple or pear	400	20
Meal 1		
Half portion of Fibre-Filler with milk from		
allowance		
An orange from allowance		
Meal 2		
1 Prewett's Muesli Fruit Bar		

	Calories	Fibre (g)
125g carton Waistline Reduced Calorie Fruit Yogurt, any flavour	200	3·5

Meal 3

1 frozen beefburger, well grilled and served in a 2oz (55g) wholemeal bap or soft roll, spread with 1oz (30g) sweet pickle; serve with a small bunch of watercress and 1 medium tomato	295	7

Meal 4

Remaining portion of Fibre-Filler with milk from allowance

2 Energen F-Plan Diet Brancrisps, each spread with 1 tablespoon Waistline Low Calorie Vegetable Spread, any flavour, and topped with 1 medium tomato, sliced	85	2

Meal 5

1 chicken leg joint (8oz, 225g raw weight), grilled and skin removed
4oz (115g) canned sweetcorn, drained
4oz (115g) Brussels sprouts, boiled

An apple or pear from allowance	270	9·5

TOTAL	1,250	42

1,250 CALORIE MENU   **5**

	Calories	Fibre (g)
Daily allowance: Fibre-Filler (p. 24), ½ pint (285ml) skimmed milk, an orange and an apple or pear	400	20

	Calories	Fibre (g)

Meal 1
Half portion of Fibre-Filler with milk from
allowance

1 large thin slice (1½oz, 35g) wholemeal
bread, toasted and spread with ¼oz (7g)
low-fat spread and 1 level teaspoon honey
or marmalade   115   3

Meal 2
4oz (115g) cottage cheese (natural or with
chives, or with onions and peppers, or with
pineapple)
Coleslaw: 2oz (55g) finely shredded white
cabbage, mixed with 2oz (55g) grated carrot,
½oz (15g) raisins and 1 tablespoon
low-calorie salad dressing   200   4

Meal 3
4oz (115g) canned pineapple slices in
natural juice
2oz (55g) vanilla ice-cream
2 level tablespoons Toasted Bran
(Serve pineapple with ice-cream topped
with bran.)   195   3

Meal 4
2 pork sausages, grilled
4oz (115g) baked beans in tomato sauce

An orange from allowance   340   8

Meal 5
Remaining portion of Fibre-Filler with milk
from allowance

An apple or pear from allowance

| TOTAL | 1,250 | 38 |

1,250 CALORIE MENU   6

	Calories	Fibre (g)
Daily allowance: Fibre-Filler (p. 24), ½ pint (285ml) skimmed milk, an orange and an apple or pear	400	20

Meal 1
Half portion Fibre-Filler with milk from allowance

1 large thin slice (1½oz, 35g) wholemeal bread, toasted, spread with Marmite or yeast extract and topped with 4oz (115g) canned tomatoes — 90 — 4

Meal 2
1 egg (size 3), hard-boiled, halved and served with half a 7¼oz (206g) can Heinz Vegetable Salad, a few lettuce leaves, a few sprigs of watercress, and 1 tomato, sliced

1 Energen F-Plan Diet Brancrisp — 265 — 5

Meal 3
1 Quaker Harvest Crunch Bar, almond or peanut, served with 2 oz (55g) vanilla ice-cream and an orange from allowance — 185 — 1

Meal 4
1 bacon steak (3½oz, 100g raw weight), well grilled, served with 1 pineapple ring from can of pineapple slices in natural juice
4 oz (115g) canned sweetcorn kernels
4oz (115g) Brussels sprouts, boiled — 245 — 10

Meal 5
Remaining portion of Fibre-Filler with milk from allowance

	Calories	Fibre (g)
1 Energen F-Plan Diet Brancrisp, spread with 1 triangle (½oz, 15g) cheese spread and topped with a few slices of cucumber		
An apple or pear from allowance	65	1·5
TOTAL	1,250	41·5

1,250 CALORIE MENU 7

	Calories	Fibre (g)
Daily allowance: Fibre-Filler (p. 24), ½ pint (285ml) skimmed milk, an orange and an apple or pear	400	20
Meal 1 Half portion of Fibre-Filler with milk from allowance		
An average-sized banana (6oz, 170g)	80	3·5
Meal 2 Sardines and tomato on toast: 2 large thin slices (2½oz, 70g) wholemeal bread, toasted, each slice topped with 1 medium tomato, sliced, a pinch of dried thyme and 2 sardines in tomato sauce, heated through under the grill	390	8
Meal 3 4oz (115g) cottage cheese (natural, with chives, with onions and peppers or with pineapple) 1 large stick celery, cut into small sticks 2oz (55g) carrot, cut into sticks		
An apple or pear from allowance	125	2·5

	Calories	Fibre (g)
Meal 4		
1 pack Birds Eye Gravy and Lean Roast Chicken		
4oz (115g) frozen peas, boiled		
1oz (30g) button mushrooms, poached in a little stock or sliced and cooked with peas	255	9·5
Meal 5		
Remaining portion of Fibre-Filler with milk from allowance		
An orange from allowance		
TOTAL	1,250	43·5

1,250 CALORIE MENU 8

	Calories	Fibre (g)
Daily allowance: Fibre-Filler (p. 24), ½ pint (285 ml) skimmed milk, an orange and an apple or pear	400	20
Meal 1		
Half portion of Fibre-Filler with milk from allowance		
2 Energen F-Plan Diet Brancrisps, spread with ¼oz (7g) low-fat spread and 2 teaspoons honey	100	2
Meal 2		
170g carton Eden Vale Chicken and Sweetcorn Salad		
A small bunch of watercress		
An apple or pear from allowance	270	3

	Calories	Fibre (g)

Meal 3
1 small (25g) packet potato crisps, any
flavour
1 sachet Batchelors Slim-A-Soup, any
flavour, made up

An orange from allowance	170	3

Meal 4
Egg florentine: thaw and heat 5oz (140g)
frozen cut-leaf spinach (don't add butter),
season to taste with salt and pepper and
grated nutmeg. Place in a small ovenproof
dish. Top with 1 egg (size 3), poached,
covered with 3 level tablespoons natural
yogurt, and sprinkle over 1oz (30g) grated
Edam cheese; heat under grill until cheese
begins to melt

	230	7·5

Meal 5
Remaining portion of Fibre-Filler with milk
from allowance

An average-sized banana (6oz, 170g)	80	3·5

	Calories	Fibre (g)
TOTAL	**1,250**	**39**

1,250 CALORIE MENU		**9**

	Calories	Fibre (g)
Daily allowance: Fibre-Filler (p. 24), ½ pint (285ml) skimmed milk, an orange and an apple or pear	400	20

	Calories	fibre (g)
Meal 1		
Half portion of Fibre-Filler with milk from allowance		
125g carton Waistline Reduced Calorie Fruit Yogurt, any flavour	75	0
Meal 2		
7oz (200g) canned macaroni cheese		
2 medium tomatoes		
An apple or pear from allowance	275	2
Meal 3		
1 Quaker Harvest Crunch Bar, almond or peanut		
An average-sized banana (6oz, 170g)	170	4·5
Meal 4		
2 frozen Realeat Vegeburgers, grilled without fat		
4 oz (115g) canned baked beans in tomato sauce		
An orange from allowance	300	14
Meal 5		
Remaining portion of Fibre-Filler with milk from allowance		
1 Energen F-Plan Diet Brancrisp, spread with Marmite or yeast extract		
1 large stick celery	30	2
TOTAL	1,250	42·5

1,250 CALORIE MENU   10

	Calories	Fibre (g)
Daily allowance: Fibre-Filler (p.24), ½ pint (285ml) skimmed milk, an orange and an apple or pear	400	20

Meal 1
Half portion of Fibre-Filler with milk from allowance

1 large thin slice (1½oz, 35g) wholemeal bread, toasted, spread with ¼oz (7g) low-fat spread and 1 level teaspoon honey or marmalade	115	3

Meal 2
Cottage cheese and date sandwich: 2 large thin slices (2½oz, 70g) wholemeal bread, filled with 2oz (55g) cottage cheese mixed with 1oz (30g) stoneless dates, chopped

An orange from allowance	275	8·5

Meal 3
8oz (226g) can Koo Peach Slices in Apple Juice

2 level tablespoons low-fat natural yogurt	115	2·5

Meal 4
Mushroom omelet with vegetables: beat 2 eggs (size 3) with 2 tablespoons water, salt and pepper to taste and a pinch of dried mixed herbs. Grease a small non-stick omelet pan with ¼oz (7g) low-fat spread. Pour in the egg mixture and cook until just set. Spoon 7½oz (215g) canned sliced large mushrooms in brine (drained and heated)

	Calories	Fibre (g)
over half the omelet. Fold the other half over the mushrooms and turn out on a warmed plate. Serve with 4oz (115g) frozen mixed peas, sweetcorn and peppers, boiled		
An apple or pear from allowance	260	10·5
Meal 5 Remaining portion of Fibre-Filler with milk from allowance	85	0
Chocolate drink made from 1 rounded teaspoon drinking chocolate and 6½fl oz (185ml) skimmed milk additional to allowance		
TOTAL	1,250	44·5

KEEN COOK'S F-PLAN

F-Plan slimmers who are also keen cooks may wish to spend more time preparing their food than the majority of slimmers. If you are a keen cook (male or female) and can resist the temptation to nibble while in the kitchen, you will find plenty of choice of attractive, tasty dishes to prepare in these menus.

All the recipes are for two, since if you are going to take time preparing a dish it is more worthwhile if you are sharing it with at least one other person. The ingredients can be increased proportionally if you are feeding more than two people.

Since keen cooks usually prefer to spend most of their time preparing one main meal, these menus provide simple, light meals during the day, saving most of the calorie allowance for the main evening meal. A late afternoon snack has been included in each menu to help you avoid hunger pangs and to reduce the temptation to nibble while preparing your evening meal.

The menus are divided into three sections: 1,000 calories, 1,250 calories and 1,500 calories daily. The lower calorie menus are suitable for women and the 1,500 calorie menus are mainly for men.

SPECIAL DIET NOTES

1. As always, begin by deciding which daily calorie total will give you a satisfactory weight loss. You will find guidance on p. 26.

2. Plan at least two or three days ahead, preferably one week ahead, and arrange your shopping so that you always have the right foods available.

3. Make sure that you eat a wide variety of foods to give a balanced healthy diet – select several different menus, preferably all different, each week.

4. Make up the Fibre-Filler for your daily allowance either daily or for several days in one batch, following the recipe on p. 24.

5. Drink as much sugarless tea and coffee as you wish throughout the day as long as you use only the skimmed milk from your daily allowance. Artificial sweeteners can be used. Water and drinks labelled 'low-calorie' can also be drunk in unlimited quantities, but alcoholic drinks must be limited, see p. 285.

1,000 CALORIE MENU   1

	Calories	Fibre (g)
Daily allowance: Fibre-Filler (p. 24), ½ pint (285ml) skimmed milk, an orange and an apple or pear	400	20

Breakfast
Half portion of Fibre-Filler with milk from allowance

An orange from allowance

Lunch
Banana and honey sandwich: 2 large thin slices (1¼ oz, 35g each) wholemeal bread filled with 1 medium banana (6oz, 170g), mashed with 2 level teaspoons honey

An apple or pear from allowance   260   9·5

Late afternoon
Remaining portion Fibre-Filler with milk from allowance

Evening meal
* Stuffed Aubergine
Mixed salad: 1 tomato, quartered, a few sprigs of watercress, a few chicory leaves,

	Calories	Fibre (g)
1oz (30g) green pepper, chopped, 2–3 spring onions, chopped, with 1 tablespoon oil-free French dressing		
2 Energen F-Plan Diet Brancrisps, each spread with ½ triangle (¼oz, 7g) cheese spread and topped with mustard and cress or sliced cucumber	340	13

TOTAL	1,000	42·5

* Stuffed Aubergine

Serves 2

1 medium aubergine (12oz, 340g)
½oz (15g) low-fat spread
2oz (55g) onion, chopped
2 medium tomatoes (4oz, 115g), chopped
1 large thin slice (1¼oz, 35g) wholemeal bread
4 tablespoons skimmed milk, additional to allowance
2oz (55g) boiled lean ham, chopped
generous pinch of dried mixed herbs
salt and freshly ground pepper
1oz (30g) Cheddar cheese, grated

Preheat the oven to 180°C (350°F, gas 4). Cut the aubergine in half lengthwise and scoop out the flesh from the centre of each half using a teaspoon. Chop the flesh. Heat the low-fat spread in a saucepan and fry the chopped onion and tomatoes gently for 5 minutes. Break up the bread, place in a basin with the milk and leave to soak for 5 minutes, then squeeze dry and add to the chopped onion mixture with the chopped ham and aubergine flesh. Stir in the mixed herbs and season well with salt and pepper. Divide the mixture in half and pile into the aubergine shells. Place in an ovenproof dish and cover with foil. Bake in the oven for 1½ hours. Remove the foil and sprinkle over the grated cheese. Return to the oven for a further 15 minutes until the cheese is melted and beginning to brown. Serve hot.

1,000 CALORIE MENU 2

	Calories	Fibre (g)
Daily allowance: Fibre-Filler (p. 24), ½ pint (285ml) skimmed milk, an orange and an apple or pear	400	20

Breakfast
Half portion of Fibre-Filler with milk from allowance

Lunch
Ham salad: 2oz (55g) boiled lean ham with 1 medium tomato, 2oz (55g) Chinese leaves, shredded, a small bunch of watercress, 2oz (55g) carrot, grated, and 1 large stick celery, chopped

An apple or pear from allowance	130	5·5

Late afternoon
Remaining portion of Fibre-Filler with milk from allowance

Evening meal
* Stuffed Plaice with Lemon and Prawn Sauce
4oz (115g) broccoli, boiled
1 large thin slice (1½oz, 35g) wholemeal bread spread with ½oz, (7g) low-fat spread

An orange from allowance	470	12

TOTAL	1,000	37.5

* Stuffed Plaice with Lemon and Prawn Sauce

Serves 2

4 fillets plaice (3oz, 85g each), skinned

Stuffing

2oz (55g) wholemeal breadcrumbs
1oz (30g) onion, peeled and finely chopped
1oz (30g) carrot, peeled and finely grated
2oz (60g) mushrooms, finely chopped
juice and rind of half a lemon
a pinch of lemon thyme
salt and pepper

Sauce

½oz (15g) wholemeal flour
½oz (15g) low-fat spread
¼ pint (140ml) skimmed low-fat milk
1 tablespoon lemon juice
4oz (115g) prawns
1 teaspoon chopped fresh parsley
salt and pepper

Preheat the oven to 190°C (375°F, gas 5). Mix the stuffing ingredients together. Spread the stuffing over the fillets of plaice and fold in half. Place in an ovenproof dish, cover and bake for 20 minutes or until the fish is tender. Meanwhile, prepare the sauce: put the flour, low-fat spread and milk into a saucepan and heat gently, stirring continuously, until it comes to the boil and thickens. Add the lemon juice, prawns and parsley, and cook over a low heat for 5 minutes. Season to taste. Arrange the stuffed fillets of plaice on two serving plates and pour over the sauce.

1,000 CALORIE MENU **3**

	Calories	Fibre (g)
Daily allowance: Fibre-Filler (p. 24), ½ pint (285ml) skimmed milk, an orange and an apple or pear	400	20

	Calories	Fibre (g)

Breakfast
Half portion of Fibre-Filler with milk from
allowance

An orange from allowance

Lunch
2 Energen F-Plan Diet Brancrisps, spread
with 1oz (30g) low-fat cottage cheese
and topped with 1oz (30g) sliced
cucumber and 1oz (30g) corn relish

An apple or pear from allowance   130   3·5

Late afternoon
Remaining portion of Fibre-Filler with milk
from allowance

Evening meal
8oz (225g) slice cantaloup, honeydew or
yellow melon topped with half a glacé
cherry

* Spinach and Cheese Soufflé
4oz (115g) frozen mixed peas, sweetcorn
and peppers, boiled   470   13

TOTAL	1,000	36·5

* **Spinch and Cheese Soufflé**

Serves 2

4oz (115g) cooked or frozen (thawed) spinach, finely chopped
4oz (115g) cooked potato, mashed
2oz (55g) mature Cheddar cheese, grated
salt and freshly ground pepper

1oz (30g) wholemeal flour
1oz (30g) low-fat spread
¼ pint (140ml) skimmed low-fat milk
2 eggs (size 3), separated

Preheat the oven to 220°C (425°F, gas 7). Place the spinach, potato, cheese and salt and pepper in a bowl and mix thoroughly. Leave to one side. Put the flour, low-fat spread and milk into a small saucepan and heat gently, stirring all the time, until the sauce thickens. Remove from the heat and beat in the egg yolks, then stir in the spinach mixture. Whisk the egg whites until they form a soft peak and fold into the rest of the ingredients. Pour into a 1½ pint (850ml) soufflé dish and bake in the oven for 25–30 minutes or until it is golden brown and well risen. Serve immediately.

1,000 CALORIE MENU   4

	Calories	Fibre (g)
Daily allowance: Fibre-Filler (p. 24), ½ pint (285ml) skimmed milk, an orange and an apple or pear	400	20
Breakfast Half portion of Fibre-Filler with milk from allowance		
An orange from allowance		
Lunch Toasted cheese and date sandwich: fill 2 large thin slices (1¼ oz, 35g each) wholemeal bread with 1oz (30g) curd cheese mixed with 1oz (30g) finely chopped stoned dates. Toast the sandwich on both sides, cut into four and serve		
An apple or pear from allowance	260	8·5

	Calories	Fibre (g)
Late afternoon		
Remaining portion of Fibre-Filler with milk from allowance		
Evening meal		
* Minted Watercress and Cucumber Soup		
1 Energen F-Plan Diet Brancrisp		
8oz (225g) chicken leg joint, grilled and skin removed, served hot or cold		
* Kidney Bean, Onion and Cauliflower Salad	340	12·5
TOTAL	1,000	41

* Minted Watercress and Cucumber Soup

Serves 2

1 bunch (2oz, 55g) watercress
4oz (115g) cucumber, roughly chopped
1 small (3oz, 85g) onion, peeled and chopped
1 small (2oz, 55g) potato, peeled and cut into
   four
salt and freshly ground pepper
1 teaspoon chopped fresh mint
3 tablespoons low-fat natural yogurt

Place the watercress, cucumber, onion and potato in a medium-sized saucepan with ½ pint (285ml) water, bring to the boil. Reduce the heat and simmer for 15 minutes. Allow to cool for a few minutes than sieve or purée in a blender. Season to taste, add the mint and 2 tablespoons low-fat yogurt and stir thoroughly. Chill in the refrigerator. To serve, pour into two soup bowls and pour the remaining yogurt in a spiral pattern in the centre of each bowl of soup.

* Kidney Bean, Onion and Cauliflower Salad

Serves 2

6oz (170g) canned red kidney beans, drained and rinsed
4 spring onions, chopped
6oz (170g) raw cauliflower, broken into florets
½ clove garlic, crushed
1 tablespoon oil-free French dressing
1 tablespoon lemon juice

Mix the kidney beans, chopped spring onions and cauliflower
florets together in a salad bowl. Mix the garlic with the French
dressing and lemon juice and pour over the salad vegetables. Toss
well until thoroughly mixed. Allow to stand for 10 minutes before
serving.

1,000 CALORIE MENU 5

	Calories	Fibre (g)
Daily allowance: Fibre-Filler (p. 24), ½ pint (285ml) skimmed milk, an orange and an apple or pear	400	20
Breakfast Half portion Fibre-Filler with milk from allowance		
An orange from allowance		
Lunch 2 Energen F-Plan Diet Brancrisps, topped with 2oz (55g) cottage cheese mixed with ½oz (15g) raisins and ½oz (15g) chopped walnuts		
An apple or pear from allowance	210	4
Late afternoon Remaining portion Fibre-Filler with milk from allowance		

	Calories	Fibre (g)

Evening meal
* Kidney Risotto

| 4oz (115g) fresh or frozen (thawed) raspberries with 1 level teaspoon sugar | 390 | 17 |

| TOTAL | 1,000 | 41 |

* Kidney Risotto

Serves 2

1 teaspoon vegetable oil
3oz (85g) brown rice
1 small (3oz, 85g) onion, peeled and
  chopped
1 small (3oz, 85g) red pepper, deseeded and
  chopped
½ pint (285ml) beef stock, made from ½ beef
  stock cube
4 lamb's kidneys (8 oz, 225g), cored and chopped
4oz (115g) frozen peas, thawed
4oz (115g) courgette, thinly sliced, tossed in
  1–2 tablespoons oil-free French dressing
1 level teaspoon grated Parmesan cheese

Heat the oil in a medium-sized saucepan and gently fry the rice,
onion and pepper for 3–4 minutes. Add the beef stock and bring to
the boil. Reduce the heat and simmer for 25 minutes. Meanwhile
quickly brown the kidneys in a non-stick frying pan over a medium
heat. Add the kidneys and peas to the rice mixture and simmer for
a further 10–15 minutes or until the rice has absorbed most of the
stock. Arrange the courgette slices around the edge of two serving
plates and spoon the risotto into the centre. Sprinkle with Parmesan cheese.

1,250 CALORIE MENU   1

	Calories	Fibre (g)
Daily allowance: Fibre-Filler (p. 24), ½ pint (285ml) skimmed milk, an orange and an apple or pear	400	20

Breakfast
Half portion of Fibre-Filler with milk
from allowance

An orange from allowance

Lunch
Liver pâté and cress sandwich: 2 large thin
slices (1½oz, 35g each) wholemeal
bread, filled with 1½oz (40g) sliced liver
sausage and a thick layer of watercress
sprigs

An apple or pear from allowance   285   7

Late afternoon
Remaining portion of Fibre-Filler with
milk from allowance

Evening meal
* Soufflé Omelet Filled with Prawn,
Sweetcorn and Tomato
4oz (115g) broccoli, boiled
5oz (140g) new potatoes, boiled

2oz (55g) portion vanilla ice-cream
served with 1 medium banana (6oz, 170g),
sliced   565   15

| TOTAL | 1,250 | 42 |

* Soufflé Omelet Filled with Prawns, Sweetcorn and Tomato

Serves 2

Filling
2oz (55g) prawns
4oz (115g) canned sweetcorn kernels
1 medium (2oz, 55g) tomato, chopped
1 small (3oz, 85g) onion, peeled and chopped
a large pinch of mixed dried herbs

Omelet
3 eggs (size 3), separated
salt and freshly ground pepper
1 teaspoon vegetable oil
1½oz (45g) mature Cheddar cheese, grated

Place the prawns, sweetcorn, tomato, onion and herbs in a saucepan, cover and cook over a medium heat for 10–15 minutes or until the onion is soft. Prepare the omelet: whisk the egg yolks, 2 tablespoons warm water and salt and pepper together. Whisk the egg whites until they form soft peaks, then fold evenly into the whisked yolks. Heat the oil in a large frying pan or omelet pan and pour the egg mixture into it, spreading it out evenly. Cook gently for 5–7 minutes, until the underneath is golden brown, put under a preheated moderate grill for 4–5 minutes until the omelet is set and is lightly brown on the surface. Spoon the prawn, sweetcorn and tomato filling on top of one half of the omelet, sprinkle with the grated cheese. Fold in half and slide on to a hot plate. Cut into two portions and serve at once.

1,250 CALORIE MENU   2

	Calories	Fibre (g)
Daily allowance: Fibre-Filler (p. 24), ½ pint (285ml) skimmed milk, an orange and an apple or pear	400	20

	Calories	Fibre (g)

Breakfast
Half portion of Fibre-Filler with milk from
allowance

An orange from allowance

Lunch
2 Energen F-Plan Diet Brancrisps, topped
with 1 hard-boiled egg (size 3), chopped
and mixed with 2 tablespoons low-calorie
salad dressing, salt and pepper and ¼
carton mustard and cress

An apple or pear from allowance	180	2·5

Late afternoon
Remaining portion of Fibre-Filler with milk
from allowance

Evening meal
* Chicken and Grapes with Mushroom
Sauce
7oz (200g) potato, baked in its jacket
  (p. 31)
4oz (115g) Brussels sprouts

4oz (115g) fresh or frozen raspberries with 125g carton Waistline Reduced Calorie Fruit Yogurt, any flavour	670	21

TOTAL	1,250	43·5

* Chicken and Grapes with Mushroom Sauce

Serves 2

2 chicken pieces (8oz, 225g each)
2oz (55g) frozen sweetcorn kernels

4oz (115g) mushrooms, sliced
4fl oz (115ml) dry white wine
3½fl oz (100ml) chicken stock using ½ chicken stock cube
salt and pepper

Sauce
1oz (30g) wholemeal flour
½oz (15g) low-fat spread
salt and pepper
4oz (115g) green grapes, cut in half and deseeded

Preheat the oven to 200°C (400°F, gas 6). Remove the skin from the chicken joints and place them in an ovenproof dish with the sweetcorn, mushrooms, wine, chicken stock and salt and pepper. Cover and bake in the oven for 40–55 minutes or until the chicken is tender. Remove the chicken from the dish, place on a serving dish and keep warm. Strain the stock into a saucepan but reserve the mushrooms and sweetcorn. To the stock add the flour, low-fat spread and salt and pepper. Stir over a gentle heat until it thickens. Add the grapes, sweetcorn and mushrooms, and mix thoroughly. Pour over the chicken and serve.

1,250 CALORIE MENU 3

	Calories	Fibre (g)
Daily allowance: Fibre-Filler (p. 24), ½ pint (285ml) skimmed milk, an orange and an appple or pear	400	20
Breakfast Half portion of Fibre-Filler with milk from allowance		
1 large thin slice (1¼oz, 35g) wholemeal bread, toasted and spread with ¼oz (7g) low-fat spread and 2 level teaspoons honey or marmalade	130	3

	Calories	Fibre (g)

Lunch
7fl oz (200ml) carton Ambrosia Yogurt
Juice, raspberry, strawberry, peach or
black cherry

1 Jordans Original Crunchy Bar, Honey
& Almond

An apple or pear from allowance	270	0·5

Late afternoon
Remaining portion of Fibre-Filler with milk
from allowance

Evening meal
* Trout Kiev
8oz (225g) frozen peas, sweetcorn and
peppers

An orange from allowance	450	16·5

TOTAL	**1,250**	**40**

* Trout Kiev

Serves 2

2 trout (7oz, 200g each after gutting), cleaned
2 teaspoons vegetable oil

Stuffing
2oz (55g) canned sweetcorn kernels
2 level tablespoons ground almonds
1oz (30g) low-fat spread
1 clove garlic, crushed
2 tablespoons lemon juice

Garnish
lemon slices
½oz (15g) toasted flaked almonds

Wipe the trout. Mix all the stuffing ingredients together and use to stuff the two trout. Brush the skin with the oil and place on a foil-lined grill rack. Cook under a moderate grill for 8–10 minutes on each side or until the fish is cooked right through and the juices of the stuffing start to run out. Place on a hot serving dish and garnish with the lemon slices and toasted flaked almonds.

1,250 CALORIE MENU 4

	Calories	Fibre (g)
Daily allowance: Fibre-Filler (p. 24), ½ pint (285ml) skimmed milk, an orange and an apple or pear	400	20
Breakfast Half portion of Fibre-Filler with milk from allowance		
An orange from allowance		
Lunch * Mushrooms on Toast		
An apple or pear from allowance	250	6
Late afternoon Remaining portion of Fibre-Filler with milk from allowance		
Evening meal ½ grapefruit, decorated with ½ glacé cherry		
* Liver Stroganoff 4oz (115g) cauliflower, boiled		
* Blackberry and Apple Fool	600	12
TOTAL	1,250	38

* Mushrooms on Toast

Serves 1

2 large thin slices (1¼oz, 35g each) wholemeal bread
4oz (115g) button mushrooms
4fl oz (115ml) skimmed milk, additional to allowance
2 level teaspoons cornflour
a dash of Worcestershire sauce
salt and pepper
a few sprigs of watercress

Toast both sides of bread. Poach the mushrooms in the skimmed milk for 5 minutes. Blend the cornflour with a little cold water and stir into the mushrooms. Bring to the boil, stirring, and cook for 2 minutes until thickened. Add the Worcestershire sauce and seasoning to taste. Serve on the two slices of toast garnished with sprigs of watercress.

* Liver Stroganoff

Serves 2

1 teaspoon vegetable oil
8oz (225g) lamb's liver, cut into thin strips
1 small (3oz, 85g) onion, peeled and chopped
4oz (115g) mushrooms, sliced
¼ pint (140ml) beef stock, made from ½ beef stock cube
2 tablespoons dry sherry
3 tablespoons low-fat natural yogurt
3oz (85g) green tagliatelle or noodles, cooked and drained
chopped fresh parsley

Heat the oil in a medium-sized saucepan, add the liver and onion and fry gently for 3–4 minutes. Stir in the mushrooms, beef stock and sherry, bring to the boil. Reduce the heat and simmer for 12–15 minutes or until the liver is tender. Remove from the heat and stir in 2 tablespoons yogurt. Arrange the tagliatelle or noodles around the edges of two warmed plates and spoon the liver mixture into the centre. Garnish with the remaining yogurt and the chopped parsley.

* Blackberry and Apple Fool

Serves 2

4oz (115g) blackberries
8oz (225g) cooking apple, peeled, cored and
   sliced
1 level tablespoon sugar
two 125g cartons Waistline Reduced Calorie
   Natural Yogurt

Stew the blackberries and apple with 4 tablespoons water in a
covered pan until tender. Add the sugar and purée in a blender
with the yogurt. Serve cold.

1,250 CALORIE MENU   **5**

	Calories	Fibre (g)
Daily allowance: Fibre-Filler (p. 24), ½ pint (285ml) skimmed milk, an orange and an apple or pear	400	20
Breakfast Half portion of Fibre-Filler with milk from allowance		
Lunch 1 sachet Batchelors Slim-A-Soup, any flavour 2 Energen F-Plan Diet Brancrisps, topped with 2oz (55g) cottage cheese (natural, with chives or with onions and peppers) and 2 medium tomatoes, sliced	155	3·5
Late afternoon Remaining portion of Fibre-Filler with milk from allowance		

	Calories	Fibre (g)
Evening meal		
* Apricot Stuffed Lamb Chops		
4oz (115g) carrots, boiled		
4oz (115g) cabbage		
* Flambé Bananas	695	18
TOTAL	**1,250**	**41·5**

* **Apricot Stuffed Lamb Chops**

Serves 2

2 lean lamb loin chops (5oz, 140g each)

   Stuffing
1½oz (40g) dried apricots, finely chopped
1½oz (40g) wholemeal breadcrumbs
1oz (30g) onion, finely chopped
1oz (30g) walnuts, finely chopped
2 tablespoons beaten egg
a large pinch of dried marjoram
salt and pepper

Preheat the oven to 190°C (375°F, gas 5). Using a sharp knife cut a horizontal pocket in each chop from the fat edge towards the bone. Mix all the stuffing ingredients together. Fill the pocket in each chop with some of the stuffing. Form the remaining stuffing into small balls. Place the chops and stuffing balls into a shallow ovenproof dish. Cover and cook in the oven for 40–45 minutes or until the lamb is tender and cooked through. Serve hot.

* **Flambé Bananas**

Serves 2

2 medium bananas (6oz, 170g each)
3 tablespoons unsweetened orange juice

1 level teaspoon clear honey
¼ teaspoon ground cinnamon
1 tablespoon Grand Marnier or brandy
1oz (30g) walnuts, chopped

Place the bananas in a medium-sized saucepan or frying pan with the orange juice, honey and cinnamon. Bring to the boil, reduce the heat and simmer gently for 3–4 minutes or until the bananas are tender. Place with the juice on a serving dish. Heat the Grand Marnier or brandy, then set alight. While flaming pour over the bananas, and leave until flames die out. Sprinkle with the chopped walnuts.

1,250 CALORIE MENU 6

	Calories	Fibre (g)
Daily allowance: Fibre-Filler (p. 24), ½ pint (285ml) skimmed milk, an orange and an apple or pear	400	20

Breakfast
Half portion of Fibre-Filler with milk from allowance

An orange from allowance

Lunch
Banana, raisin and almond sandwich:
2 large thin slices (1½oz, 35g each) wholemeal bread filled with 6oz (170g) banana mashed with 2 teaspoons honey and mixed with 1oz (30g) raisins and ¼oz (7g) flaked almonds

An apple or pear from allowance	370	12·5

Late afternoon
Remaining portion of Fibre-Filler with milk from allowance

	Calories	Fibre (g)
Evening meal		
* Crab and Apple Cocktail		
6oz (170g) gammon rasher, well grilled,		
served with 1 ring pineapple, from a can		
of pineapple in natural juice, heated		
through under grill		
4oz (115g) broccoli, boiled		
4oz (115g) broad beans, boiled	480	12·5
TOTAL	1,250	45

* Crab and Apple Cocktail

Serves 2

3oz (85g) crab meat
1 medium (5oz, 140g) eating apple (additional to allowance),
  cored and chopped
1oz (30g) canned sweetcorn kernels

Dressing
1 level teaspoon tomato purée
2 dessertspoons low-calorie salad dressing
a pinch of dry mustard
1 teaspoon lemon juice
1 teaspoon skimmed low-fat milk

Garnish
a few lettuce leaves, shredded
1 medium (2oz, 55g) tomato, sliced
lemon wedges

Place the crab, apple and sweetcorn in a medium-sized bowl and mix well. Mix all the dressing ingredients together and stir into the crab mixture. Line two glass dishes with shredded lettuce and pile the crab and apple mixture on top. Garnish with the tomato and lemon. Chill.

1,250 CALORIE MENU 7

	Calories	Fibre (g)
Daily allowance: Fibre-Filler (p. 24), ½ pint (285ml) skimmed milk, an orange and an apple or pear	400	20

Breakfast
Whole portion of Fibre-Filler with milk from allowance

Lunch
Creamed mushrooms on toast: 1 large thin slice (1¼oz, 35g) wholemeal bread, toasted and topped with 7½oz (213g) can Chesswood Sliced Mushrooms in Creamed Sauce, heated and mixed with 2½ level tablespoons bran and 1 tablespoon Worcestershire sauce

An apple or pear from allowance	300	8

Late afternoon
1 Jordans Original Crunchy Bar, Honey & Coconut

An orange from allowance	145	1

Evening meal
* Tropical Melon

* Chicken and Fruit Salad

2 Energen F-Plan Diet Brancrisps, spread with ¼oz (7g) low-fat spread	405	8

TOTAL	1,250	37

* Tropical Melon

Serves 2

1lb 4oz (570g) water melon, rind and pips removed, flesh cut into 1in (2·5cm) cubes

1 tablespoon white rum
1 tablespoon unsweetened orange juice
2 level teaspoons desiccated coconut

Place the melon in a mixing bowl with the rum and orange juice and mix well. Cover and leave to stand for 1 hour in a cool place. Divide equally between two glass dishes and sprinkle with the coconut. Serve chilled.

* Chicken and Fruit Salad

Serves 2

6oz (170g) cooked chicken with all skin removed
2 rings pineapple from a can of pineapple rings in natural juice
4oz (115g) green grapes, halved and pips removed
150g carton low-fat natural yogurt
1 tablespoon lemon juice
salt and pepper
a few lettuce leaves
4oz (115g) cucumber, sliced
4oz (115g) canned sweetcorn kernels

Dice the chicken into bite-sized pieces and chop the pineapple rings. Place in a bowl with the grapes. Mix the yogurt with the lemon juice and season well with salt and pepper. Stir into the chicken mixture. Arrange a bed of lettuce leaves on two plates, divide the chicken and fruit salad equally between the two plates and pile into the centre. Arrange a ring of sliced cucumber around the edge and then spoon a thin ring of sweetcorn kernels on top of the cucumber slices.

1,250 CALORIE MENU   8

	Calories	Fibre (g)
Daily allowance: Fibre-Filler (p.24), ½ pint (285ml) skimmed milk, an orange and an apple or pear	400	20

	Calories	Fibre (g)
Breakfast		
Half portion of Fibre-Filler with milk from allowance		
An average-sized banana (6oz, 170g)	80	3·5
Lunch		
8oz (225g) canned baked beans in tomato sauce heated and topped with ½oz (15g) Edam cheese, grated		
An orange from allowance	205	16·5
Late afternoon		
Remaining portion of Fibre-Filler with milk from allowance		
Evening meal		
* Steak Kebabs		
Green salad: a few lettuce leaves, a few slices of cucumber, a small bunch of watercress		
An apple or pear from allowance	565	8
TOTAL	1,250	50

* Steak Kebabs

Serves 2

Marinade
1 tablespoon vegetable oil
2 tablespoons red wine
1 tablespoon low-calorie salad dressing

8oz (225g) rump steak, cut into ¾in (2cm) cubes
6 button onions or spring onion bulbs (2oz, 55g)
2 medium (4oz, 115g) tomatoes, each cut into four

3oz (85g) button mushrooms
1 small (3oz, 85g) green pepper, cut into 1in (2·5cm) pieces
6 bay leaves

To serve
4oz (115g) brown rice, boiled
2oz (55g) canned sweetcorn kernels, heated

Mix the marinade ingredients together. Place the cubes of steak in the marinade and leave, covered, for approximately 1 hour. Then thread the steak on to two long or four medium skewers, alternating with the onions, tomato, mushrooms, green pepper and bay leaves. Cook under a preheated moderate grill for 15 minutes, turning several times and brushing with the marinade. Mix the rice with the sweetcorn and spoon on to a warm serving dish. Place the kebabs on top and serve.

1,250 CALORIE MENU 9

	Calories	Fibre (g)
Daily allowance Fibre-Filler (p. 24), ½ pint (285ml) skimmed milk, an orange and an apple or pear	400	20

Breakfast
Whole portion of Fibre-Filler with milk from allowance

Lunch
Mushroom scramble on toast: poach 2oz (55g) mushrooms, sliced, in 2fl oz (55ml) skimmed milk (additional to allowance) in a saucepan. Add 2 eggs (size 3), beaten, with salt and pepper and cook gently, stirring, until the eggs are creamy. Serve on 1 large thin slice (1¼oz, 35g) wholemeal bread, toasted

	Calories	Fibre (g)
An orange from allowance	265	4·5

	Calories	Fibre (g)
Late afternoon		
1 small packet (25g) potato crisps		
1 apple or pear from allowance	130	3
Evening meal		
* Ham with Bean Salad		
* Fruited Orange Sorbet	455	15·5
TOTAL	**1,250**	**43**

* Ham with Bean Salad

Serves 2

6oz (170g) boiled lean ham, sliced
4oz (115g) French beans
2 large sticks celery, chopped
1oz (30g) onion, finely chopped
15½oz (440g) canned red kidney beans, drained
1 small green pepper (3oz, 85g), seeds removed and sliced
5 tablespoons oil-free French dressing
salt and pepper
a small bunch of watercress

Remove all visible fat from the meat. Cook the French beans in salted water until just tender, drain and rinse under cold water to cool. Cut the French beans into bite-sized pieces and mix in a salad bowl with the celery, onion, red kidney beans and green pepper. Add the dressing and salt and pepper to taste and mix well. Serve the salad with the sliced ham and garnish with watercress.

* Fruited Orange Sorbet

Serves 2

¼ pint (140ml) unsweetened orange juice *or* unsweetened passion fruit and orange juice

1oz (30g) granulated sugar
1oz (30g) sultanas
1 large (8oz, 225g) orange
1 egg white

To decorate
1 glacé cherry, halved
2 mint leaves

Place the orange juice, sugar and sultanas into a saucepan and heat until the sugar dissolves. Allow to cool. Cut the orange in half and cut out the flesh, reserve the two halves of orange skin. Purée the orange flesh in a blender and stir into the orange juice. Pour into a freezer container and freeze until granular. Beat with a fork. Whisk the egg white until it forms soft peaks, then fold in the orange mixture. Return to the freezer container and freeze until hard. To serve, spoon into the two halves of orange skin. Decorate each with half a glacé cherry and a mint leaf.

1,500 CALORIE MENU 1

	Calories	Fibre (g)
Daily allowance: Fibre-Filler (p. 24), ½ pint (285ml) skimmed milk, an orange and an apple or pear	400	20

Breakfast
Half portion of Fibre-Filler with milk from allowance

| 1 egg (size 3), boiled and served with 1 large thin slice (1½oz, 35g) wholemeal bread, spread with ¼oz (7g) low-fat spread | 180 | 3 |

Lunch
Cheese and pineapple on toast: 1 large thin slice (1½oz, 35g) wholemeal bread, toasted,

	Calories	Fibre (g)

and covered with 1oz (30g) grated Cheddar
cheese and 1 ring pineapple from a can of
pineapple in natural juice. Heat through
under a hot grill until cheese has melted.
Garnish with a few sprigs of watercress

	Calories	Fibre (g)
An apple or pear from allowance	225	3·5

Late afternoon
Remaining portion of Fibre-Filler with milk
from allowance

Evening meal
* Tuna Pasties
* Orange and Watercress Salad

150g carton low-fat raspberry-flavoured yogurt served with 6oz (170g) banana, peeled and sliced	695	11·5
TOTAL	1,500	40

* Tuna Pasties

Serves 2

Pastry
4oz (115g) wholemeal flour
pinch of salt
1½oz (45g) low-fat spread
½oz (15g) margarine

Filling
3½oz (100g) canned tuna in brine, drained and
  flaked
1½oz (45g) mature Cheddar cheese, grated
1 teaspoon tomato purée

1 teaspoon low-calorie salad dressing
1 medium (2oz, 55g) tomato, chopped
1 medium (5oz, 140g) eating apple, additional to allowance,
  cored and chopped
freshly ground pepper

For brushing
½ teaspoon salt in 3 tablespoons warm water

Preheat the oven to 200°C (400°F, gas 6). Place the wholemeal flour, salt, low-fat spread and margarine in a mixing bowl and rub the ingredients together using the fingertips until the mixture resembles breadcrumbs. Mix in enough cold water to form a soft dough, lightly knead, then cut into two. Roll out each half to a 7in (17·5cm) circle. Mix all the filling ingredients together. Divide the filling equally between the two pastry circles. Damp the edges with water, then bring up the edges to meet in the middle to form a pasty shape. Flute the joined edges using a finger and a thumb. Place on a baking sheet and brush with the salt and water. Bake in the oven for 25–30 minutes or until the pastry is golden brown. Serve hot or cold.

* Orange and Watercress Salad

Serves 2

2 medium-sized oranges (1 orange from allowance)
a large bunch of watercress
2 tablespoons lemon juice
salt and pepper
a few lettuce leaves

Cut the peel and pith off the orange using a sharp stainless steel knife. Cut the orange segments out from the membranes. Divide the watercress into sprigs, discarding any yellowed leaves, and mix with the orange segments, lemon juice and seasoning to taste. Line two individual salad bowls with lettuce leaves and spoon in the orange and watercress salad.

1,500 CALORIE MENU 2

	Calories	Fibre (g)
Daily allowance: Fibre-Filler (p. 24), ½ pint (285ml) skimmed milk, an orange and an apple or pear	400	20

Breakfast
Half portion of Fibre-Filler with milk from allowance

1 large thin slice (1½oz, 35g) wholemeal bread, toasted and spread with ¼oz (7g) low-fat spread and 2 level teaspoons honey or marmalade 130 3

Lunch
2oz (55g) wholemeal bap or lunch roll, split and filled with 1 hard-boiled egg (size 3), chopped and mixed with 1 tablespoon low-calorie salad dressing and ¼ carton mustard and cress

1 large digestive biscuit

An apple or pear from allowance 295 6

Late afternoon
Remaining portion of Fibre-Filler with milk from allowance

Evening meal
* Vegetable and Ham Gougère
* Ice-cream and Orange Sundae 675 12·5

TOTAL	1,500	41·5

*Vegetable and Ham Gougère

Serves 2

Filling
7½oz (215g) canned butter beans, drained
2oz (55g) frozen peas, boiled
4oz (115g) cauliflower, broken into small florets and boiled
2oz (55g) carrot, sliced and boiled
2oz (55g) mushrooms, sliced
2oz (55g) boiled ham, chopped
1oz (30g) wholemeal flour
1oz (30g) low-fat spread
7fl oz (200ml) skimmed low-fat milk
salt and freshly ground pepper
1oz (30g) mature Cheddar cheese, grated

Choux pastry
1½oz (40g) low-fat spread
2oz (55g) wholemeal flour
1 egg (size 3), beaten

Preheat the oven to 220°C (425°F, gas 7). Place the butter beans, peas, cauliflower, carrot, mushrooms and ham into a bowl and mix well. Put the flour, low-fat spread, milk and salt and pepper into a small pan. Stir over a gentle heat until it thickens. Add the vegetable and ham mixture and mix thoroughly. Pour into a 1½ pint (850ml) ovenproof dish, sprinkle with the grated cheese and leave to one side. To make the choux pastry, put 3½fl oz (100ml) water and the low-fat spread into a small saucepan; bring to the boil. Stir in the flour all at once and beat well until the mixture leaves the sides of the saucepan clean. Remove from the heat and gradually beat in the egg. Using a ½in (1cm) nozzle, pipe the choux pastry round the edge of the filling. Bake in the hot oven for 15 minutes, then reduce the heat to 190°C (375°F, gas 5) and cook for a further 15 minutes, or until the cheese is beginning to brown. Serve hot.

* Ice-cream and Orange Sundae

Serves 2

4oz (115g) vanilla ice-cream
2 medium oranges (1 from allowance), segmented
½oz (15g) Jordans Original Crunchy with Bran and Apple

Divide the ice-cream in scoops equally between two sundae glasses
in layers, with the orange segments and Original Crunchy with
Bran and Apple. Serve at once.

1,500 CALORIE MENU   3

	Calories	Fibre (g)
Daily allowance: Fibre-Filler (p. 24), ½ pint (285ml) skimmed milk, an orange and an apple or pear	400	20

Breakfast
Whole portion of Fibre-Filler with milk from
allowance

Lunch
Cottage cheese and coleslaw salad: 4oz
(115g) low-fat cottage cheese (natural,
with onion and peppers or with pineapple),
served with 8oz (226g) carton Eden Vale
Coleslaw with Low Calorie Dressing and
with 1 medium tomato, quartered

An orange from allowance	235	5

Late afternoon
1 small packet (25g) potato crisps

An apple or pear from allowance	130	3

	Calories	Fibre (g)

Evening meal
½ grapefruit decorated with ½ glacé cherry
* Gammon with Somerset Sauce
4oz (115g) broad beans, boiled
4oz (115g) cauliflower, boiled

2 Energen F-Plan Diet Brancrisps with
1½oz (45g) Camembert, Brie or Edam cheese
1 large stick celery

	Calories	Fibre (g)
	735	13
TOTAL	1,500	41

---

*Gammon with Somerset Sauce

Serves 2

2 gammon rashers or steaks (6oz, 170g each)

Sauce
5fl oz (140ml) dry cider and 4 tablespoons water
1 small (6oz, 170g) cooking apple, cored and chopped
1 oz (30g) raisins
4 cloves
¼ teaspoon dry mustard
1 level teaspoon cornflour, blended with 1 teaspoon water

Garnish
8 slices of a red eating apple dipped in lemon juice,
    additional to allowance

Make cuts in the fat of the gammon rashers or steaks to prevent curling during cooking. Grill under a preheated moderate grill for 8–10 minutes on each side or until the fat is well browned. Meanwhile, make the sauce: put all the ingredients into a medium-sized saucepan and bring to the boil, stirring continuously. Reduce the heat and simmer for 15 minutes. Arrange the gammon rashers on a serving dish and spoon the sauce over them. Garnish with the sliced apple.

1,500 CALORIE MENU 4

	Calories	Fibre (g)
Daily allowance: Fibre-Filler (p. 24), ½ pint (285ml) skimmed milk, an orange and an apple or pear	400	20

Breakfast
Whole portion of Fibre-Filler with milk from allowance

Lunch Cottage cheese and carrot sandwich: 2 large thin slices (1½oz, 35g each) wholemeal bread filled with 2oz (55g) cottage cheese with chives mixed with 2oz (55g) carrot, grated, and 1 tablespoon low-calorie salad dressing	235	7·5

Late afternoon
Jordans Original Crunchy Bar, Honey & Coconut

An orange from allowance	145	1

Evening meal 1 chicken leg joint (8oz, 225g raw weight), baked in the oven and skin removed before serving 7oz (200g) potato baked in its jacket (see p. 31), split and topped with 1 tablespoon cottage cheese with chives mixed with 2 tablespoons oil-free French dressing 4oz (115g) frozen mixed peas, sweetcorn and peppers, boiled		
* Lemon Cheesecake	720	14·5

TOTAL	1,500	43

* Lemon Cheesecake

Serves 2

Base
3 large wheatmeal digestive biscuits, crushed
½oz (15g) low-fat spread

Filling
2oz (55g) low-fat cottage cheese, sieved
2 level tablespoons caster sugar
1 egg (size 3), separated
juice and grated rind of ½ lemon
2 level teaspoons powdered gelatine
4 tablespoons low-fat natural yogurt

Decoration
2 kiwi fruit, peeled and sliced

Place the crushed biscuits and low-fat spread in a saucepan and heat until they are thoroughly mixed. Divide equally between two individual glass dishes or tip into a 6in (15cm) flan ring on a baking tray; press down well. Leave in a cool place. Beat together the cottage cheese, sugar and egg yolk until smooth, add the lemon juice and grated rind. Dissolve the gelatine in 2 tablespoons water in a heatproof bowl over hot water. Stir into the cheese mixture with the yogurt. Whisk the egg white until it forms soft peaks, then fold into the other ingredients and pour over the biscuit base. Leave in a cool place to set. Decorate with sliced kiwi fruit.

1,500 CALORIE MENU **5**

	Calories	Fibre (g)
Daily allowance: Fibre-Filler (p. 24), ¼ pint (285ml) skimmed milk, an orange and an apple or pear	400	20

	Calories	Fibre (g)

Breakfast
Whole portion of Fibre-Filler with milk from
allowance

Lunch
* Minestrone Soup
2oz (55g) wholemeal lunch roll or bap,
spread with ½oz (7g) low-fat spread

An apple or pear from allowance	360	15

Late afternoon
1 large thin slice (1½oz. 35g) wholemeal
bread, spread with ½oz (7g) low-fat spread
and 2 level teaspoons honey

An orange from allowance	130	3

Evening meal
8oz (225g) rump steak, grilled and all fat
trimmed off
Mixed salad: few lettuce leaves, 1oz (30g)
cucumber, sliced, 1 medium tomato, sliced,
1oz (30g) green pepper, sliced, 1oz (30g)
onion rings, a few sprigs of watercress and
1 tablespoon oil-free French dressing

* Raspberry Sundae	610	11

TOTAL	1,500	49

* Minestrone

Serves 2

2oz (55g) onion, coarsely grated or finely chopped
4oz (115g) carrot, coarsely grated
4oz (115g) parsnip, coarsely grated

1 chicken stock cube
½ pint (285ml) tomato juice
2oz (55g) wholewheat macaroni
4oz (115g) cabbage, finely shredded
salt and pepper
1 tablespoon chopped fresh parsley
2 level tablespoons grated Parmesan cheese

Put the onion, carrot and parsnip into a saucepan. Dissolve the chicken stock cube in ½ pint (285ml) boiling water and add to the vegetables in the pan with the tomato juice and macaroni. Bring to the boil, stir well, cover and simmer gently for 15 minutes. Add the cabbage, bring back to the boil and cook, covered, for a further 5–10 minutes until the cabbage is tender. Season to taste with salt and pepper and stir in the chopped parsley. Serve in two soup bowls and sprinkle 1 tablespoon cheese over each bowl. Serve hot.

* Raspberry Sundae

Serves 2

Jelly
8oz (225g) raspberries, fresh or frozen
½oz (15g) soft brown sugar
2 level teaspoons powdered gelatine, dissolved in 2 tablespoons water

Topping
3½oz (90g) petit suisse cheese
3 tablespoons low-fat natural yogurt
1 level dessertspoon caster sugar

Place the raspberries, sugar and 7fl oz (200ml) water in a small saucepan and bring to the boil. Reduce the heat and simmer gently for 2–3 minutes. Remove from the heat and cool for a few minutes. Stir in the dissolved gelatine and pour into two sundae glasses. Leave to set, tilted on one side so the jelly sets at an angle. Meanwhile blend the petit suisse cheese, yogurt and caster sugar together. When the raspberry jelly is set, spoon half the topping into each glass on top of the jelly. Serve at once.

CANNED AND PACKAGED F-PLAN

As the title suggests, these menus contain a large number of ready-prepared canned and packaged convenience foods for those whose lifestyle leaves little time or inclination for food preparation. While they follow most of the basic F-Plan diet rules, the daily allowance has been adjusted so that packaged cereals can be used in place of Fibre-Filler to cut out the need to weigh out and make up the ingredients. Adequate food storage space, especially a food freezer, is an advantage when following these menus unless you can shop frequently.

To enable both men and women to use these menus, a choice of menus providing 1,000 calories, 1,250 calories and 1,500 calories daily has been given. All you have to do is to decide which daily calorie total will suit you best, i.e. give you the most satisfactory weight loss. You could find that if you are strict from Monday to Friday, i.e. selecting menus from the 1,000 calories section, you will be able to allow yourself to be a little more generous at the weekends and choose menus from the 1,250 calories or 1,500 calories section, and still achieve a satisfactory weight loss.

If you find that you long for the occasional alcoholic drink or bar of chocolate and can only stick to a diet which allows you to indulge occasionally, turn to the 1,500 calories menus. However, it may be necessary to limit strictly the number of days when you allow yourself an intake of 1,500 calories if your weight loss is slow.

SPECIAL DIET NOTES

1. Select the menus for at least one week at a time so that you can plan the shopping and always have the right foods available.

2. The daily allowance for all the 1,000 calories and 1,250 calories menus includes one tub Energen F-Plan Crunchy Bran Muesli in place of Fibre-Filler. The 1,500 calories menus have a high-fibre breakfast cereal with dried fruit for breakfast and no Fibre-Filler has been included in the daily allowance.

3. All the menus include ½ pint (285ml) skimmed milk and two whole fresh fruits (one orange and an apple or pear) in the daily allowance.

4. Use your skimmed milk allowance with the Crunchy Bran Muesli or cereal and in tea and coffee.

5. Tea and coffee are unlimited as long as you don't add sugar (artificial sweeteners can be used). In addition you can drink unlimited amounts of those drinks labelled 'low-calorie', and water.

6. The menus are divided into breakfast, a light meal, a main meal and an any-time snack or drink. You can eat these meals in any order you wish throughout the day, but eat *only* those meals/snacks and/or drinks included in your chosen menu.

1,000 CALORIE MENU   1

	Calories	Fibre (g)
Daily allowance: 2 tubs Energen F-Plan Crunchy Bran Muesli, ½ pint (285ml) skimmed milk, two items of fruit	420	20
Breakfast 1 tub Energen F-Plan Crunchy Bran Muesli with milk from allowance		
Light meal 10·6oz (300g) can Heinz Lentil Soup 1 Allinson's wholemeal snack roll (1½oz, 42g) An apple or pear from allowance	270	9·5
Main meal Individual pack of Birds Eye Gravy & Lean Roast Chicken		

	Calories	Fibre (g)
8oz (225g) Birds Eye Cauliflower, Peas & Carrots		
An orange from allowance	270	9·5
Any-time snacks 1 tub of Energen F-Plan Crunchy Bran Muesli with milk from allowance		
1 Boots Second Nature Wholemeal Hazelnut Biscuit	40	0·5
TOTAL	1,000	39·5

1,000 CALORIE MENU   2

	Calories	Fibre (g)
Daily allowance: 2 tubs Energen F-Plan Crunchy Bran Muesli, ½ pint (285ml) skimmed milk, two items of fruit	420	20
Breakfast 1 tub Energen F-Plan Crunchy Bran Muesli with milk from allowance		
An orange from allowance		
Light meal 2 large thin slices (1½oz, 35g each) wholemeal bread filled with the contents of a 1¼oz (35g) pot of Princes Crab Pâté and 1oz (30g) watercress		
2oz (55g) carrot sticks	215	8·5

	Calories	Fibre (g)
Main meal		
3oz (85g) sliced corned beef		
8oz (226g) carton Eden Vale Coleslaw in Vinaigrette		
Mixed salad: a few lettuce leaves, 1oz (30g) cucumber, sliced, 2 average tomatoes, sliced, 2 spring onions, chopped, 1oz (30g) green or red pepper, sliced and chopped with 1 tablespoon Waistline Oil-Free French Dressing		
2 Energen F-Plan Diet Brancrisps, spread with ½oz (7g) low-fat spread	365	11
Any-time snacks		
1 tub Energen F-Plan Crunchy Bran Muesli with milk from allowance		
An apple or pear from allowance		
TOTAL	1,000	39·5

1,000 CALORIE MENU   3

	Calories	Fibre (g)
Daily allowance: 2 tubs Energen F-Plan Crunchy Bran Muesli, ½ pint (285ml) skimmed milk, two items of fruit	420	20
Breakfast		
1 tub Energen F-Plan Crunchy Bran Muesli with milk from allowance		
1 large thin slice (1½oz, 35g) wholemeal		

	Calories	Fibre (g)
bread, toasted and spread with ¼oz (7g) low-fat spread and Marmite or savoury yeast extract	105	3

Light meal
1 large thin slice (1¼oz, 35g) wholemeal
bread, toasted and topped with 8oz (225g)

canned baked beans in tomato sauce	235	19·5

Main meal
1 packet Birds Eye Chicken & Mushroom
Casserole
4oz (115g) frozen Brussels sprouts, boiled
4oz (115g) canned new potatoes

An orange from allowance	240	6·5

Any-time snacks
1 tub Energen F-Plan Crunchy
Bran Muesli with milk from
allowance

TOTAL	**1,000**	**49**

1,000 CALORIE MENU 4

	Calories	Fibre (g)
Daily allowance: 2 tubs Energen F-Plan Crunchy Bran Muesli, ½ pint (285ml) skimmed milk, two items of fruit	420	20

Breakfast
Both tubs of Energen F-Plan Crunchy
Bran Muesli with milk from allowance

	Calories	Fibre (g)
Light meal		
2 Energen F-Plan Diet Brancrisps, spread with the contents of a 1·23oz (35g) pot of Shippams Chicken & Bacon Country Pot Paste and each topped with an average-sized tomato, sliced, and a little mustard and cress		
An apple or pear from allowance	120	4
Main meal		
13·6oz (385g) pack Marco & Carlo Spaghetti Bolognese (whole pack)		
4oz (115g) frozen peas, boiled		
An average-sized banana (6oz, 170g)	460	14
Any-time snack		
An orange from allowance		
TOTAL	1,000	38

1,000 CALORIE MENU 5

	Calories	Fibre (g)
Daily allowance: 2 tubs Energen F-Plan Crunchy Bran Muesli, ½ pint (285ml) skimmed milk, two items of fruit	420	20

Breakfast
Both tubs Energen F-Plan Crunchy Bran Muesli with milk from allowance

	Calories	Fibre (g)
Light meal		
4oz (115g) carton cottage cheese with onion and peppers		
8oz (226g) carton Eden Vale Coleslaw in Vinaigrette		
An apple or pear from allowance	190	6·5
Main meal		
15oz (425g) can Campbell's Main Course Pea & Ham Soup		
1 Energen F-Plan Diet Brancrisp		
An orange from allowance	375	10·5
Any-time snacks		
2oz (55g) carrot sticks		
1 large stick celery	15	2·5
TOTAL	**1,000**	**39·5**

1,000 CALORIE MENU 6

	Calories	Fibre (g)
Daily allowance: 2 tubs Energen F-Plan Crunchy Bran Muesli, ½ pint (285ml) skimmed milk, two items of fruit	420	20

Breakfast
1 tub Energen F-Plan Crunchy Bran Muesli with milk from allowance

Light meal
150g carton fruit-flavoured low-fat yogurt

	Calories	Fibre (g)
1 Quaker Harvest Crunch Bar, almond or peanut		
An orange from allowance	210	1

Main meal
1 egg (size 3), poached
2 rashers streaky bacon, grilled crisp
8oz (225g) canned baked beans in tomato
sauce

An apple or pear from allowance	340	16·5

Any-time snacks
1 tub Energen F-Plan Crunchy
Bran Muesli with milk from
allowance

1 Energen F-Plan Diet Brancrisp, spread with Marmite or yeast extract	30	1·5

TOTAL	1,000	39

1,000 CALORIE MENU 7

	Calories	Fibre (g)
Daily allowance: 2 tubs Energen F-Plan Crunchy Bran Muesli, ½ pint (285ml) skimmed milk, two items of fruit	420	20

Breakfast
1 tub Energen F-Plan Crunchy Bran
Muesli with milk from allowance

	Calories	Fibre (g)
Light meal 15·3oz (435g) can Heinz Vegetable & Lentil Big Soup		
An apple or pear from allowance	210	9
Main meal 1 pack Birds Eye Cod in Cheese Sauce 4oz (115g) Birds Eye Peas, Sweetcorn & Peppers, boiled Half medium pack Smash Potato Pieces, made up with boiling water (no butter)	360	12
Any-time snacks 1 tub Energen F-Plan Crunchy Bran Muesli with milk from allowance		
2 large sticks celery	10	2
TOTAL	1,000	43

1,250 CALORIE MENU   1

	Calories	Fibre (g)
Daily allowance: 2 tubs Energen F-Plan Crunchy Bran Muesli, ½ pint (285ml) skimmed milk, two items of fruit	420	20
Breakfast Both tubs of Energen F-Plan Crunchy Bran Muesli with milk from allowance		
Light meal Peanut salad sandwich: 2 large thin slices		

	Calories	Fibre (g)
(1½oz, 35g each) wholemeal bread spread with 1oz (30g) peanut butter and filled with 1 lettuce leaf, 1 tomato, sliced, a few slices of cucumber and a few sprigs of watercress		
An orange from allowance	340	9·5

Main meal

	Calories	Fibre (g)
15oz (425g) can Campbell's Steak & Kidney Stew		
8oz (225g) Birds Eye Cauliflower, Peas & Carrots		
Half packet Smash Potato Pieces, made up with boiling water (no butter)	425	14

Any-time snacks

	Calories	Fibre (g)
1 Energen F-Plan Diet Brancrisp, spread with 1 triangle cheese spread		
An apple or pear from allowance	65	1·5

TOTAL	1,250	45

1,250 CALORIE MENU 2

	Calories	Fibre (g)
Daily allowance: 2 tubs Energen F-Plan Crunchy Bran Muesli, ½ pint (285ml) skimmed milk, two items of fruit	420	20

Breakfast
Both tubs Energen F-Plan Crunchy Bran Muesli with milk from allowance

An orange from allowance

	Calories	Fibre (g)
Light meal 1 large thin slice (1½oz, 35g) wholemeal bread topped with 1oz (30g) Cheddar cheese, grated and mixed with 1oz (30g) sweet pickle and grilled until cheese melts 2 average-sized tomatoes a small bunch of watercress		
An apple or pear from allowance	250	6
Main meal 10½oz (300g) Findus Cottage Pie 4oz (115g) frozen peas, boiled 150g carton low-fat fruit-flavoured yogurt	500	9
Any-time snack 1 piece Allinson Wholemeal Shortbread	80	1
TOTAL	1,250	36

1,250 CALORIE MENU   3

	Calories	Fibre (g)
Daily allowance: 2 tubs Energen F-Plan Crunchy Bran Muesli, ½ pint (285ml) skimmed milk, two items of fruit	420	20
Breakfast Both tubs Energen F-Plan Crunchy Bran Muesli with milk from allowance		
Light meal 10·6oz (300g) can Heinz Pea & Ham Soup 2 Energen F-Plan Diet Brancrisps		
An apple or pear from allowance	245	9·5

	Calories	Fibre (g)

Main Meal
1 Findus Savoury Barbecue Beef French
Bread Pizza
Salad: a few lettuce leaves, 1 tomato, sliced,
1oz (30g) cucumber, sliced, a small bunch of
watercress, 1oz (30g) green pepper, sliced,
dressed with 1 tablespoon low-calorie oil-free
French dressing

10oz (283g) can John West Peach Slices in Fruit Juice	540	8·5

Any-time snacks
An orange from allowance

1 Boots Second Nature Bran Biscuit	45	1·5

TOTAL	1,250	39·5

1,250 CALORIE MENU   4

	Calories	Fibre (g)
Daily allowance: 2 tubs Energen F-Plan Crunchy Bran Muesli, ½ pint (285ml) skimmed milk, two items of fruit	420	20

Breakfast
Both tubs Energen F-Plan Crunchy Bran
Muesli with milk from allowance

Light meal
Bacon and green pepper sandwich: 2 slices
(1¼oz, 35g each) wholemeal bread filled with
1⅞oz (53g) pot Princes Smokey Bacon
Spread and 1½oz (45g) chopped green pepper

An orange from allowance	280	6·5

	Calories	Fibre (g)
Main meal		
1 Findus All Beef Quarter Pounder (beefburger), well grilled		
Half 10·7oz (304g) can Batchelor's Mushy Peas		
3½oz (100g) canned small whole mushrooms in brine		
150g carton low-fat fruit-flavoured yogurt	460	12·5
Any-time snacks		
An apple or pear from allowance		
1 Quaker Harvest Crunch Bar, almond or peanut	90	1
TOTAL	1,250	40

1,250 CALORIE MENU   5

	Calories	Fibre (g)
Daily allowance: 2 tubs Energen F-Plan Crunchy Bran Muesli, ½ pint (285ml) skimmed milk, two items of fruit	420	20

Breakfast
Both tubs Energen F-Plan Crunchy Bran Muesli with milk from allowance

Light meal
Creamy mushrooms on toast: 1 large thin slice (1¼oz, 35g) wholemeal bread, toasted and topped with 7½oz (215g) canned sliced mushrooms in creamed sauce, mixed with 1 level tablespoon bran and 1 tablespoon

	Calories	Fibre (g)
Worcestershire sauce and heated through a small bunch of watercress		
An apple or pear from allowance	285	7

Main meal
2 sausalatas from 10oz (283g) can Granose
Sausalatas, grilled
Half medium packet Smash Potato Pieces,
made up without butter
8oz (225g) Birds Eye Peas & Baby Carrots

150g carton low-fat natural yogurt with 1 level teaspoon honey or soft brown sugar	395	22

Any-time snacks
1 choc ice (chocolate covered ice-cream bar)
or 1 Cadbury's Fudge Bar

An orange from allowance	150	0

TOTAL	1,250	49

1,250 CALORIE MENU   6

	Calories	Fibre (g)
Daily allowance: 2 tubs Energen F-Plan Crunchy Bran Muesli, ½ pint (285ml) skimmed milk, two items of fruit	420	20

Breakfast
1 tub Energen F-Plan Crunchy Bran
Muesli with milk from allowance

1 egg (size 3), poached and served on

	Calories	Fibre (g)
1 large thin slice (1½oz, 35g) wholemeal bread, toasted	155	3
Light meal 2 sardines in tomato sauce Half 7½oz (206g) can Heinz Vegetable Salad A few lettuce leaves 1 average-sized tomato		
An apple or pear from allowance	270	3·5
Main meal 1 pack Birds Eye Liver with Onion & Gravy Half medium packet Smash Potato Pieces, made up without butter Half 10oz (283g) can Hartley's or Smedley's broad beans		
An orange from allowance	350	9
Any-time snacks 1 tub Energen F-Plan Crunchy Bran Muesli with milk from allowance		
1 small (4oz, 115g) banana	55	2·5
TOTAL	1,250	38

1,250 CALORIE MENU 7

	Calories	Fibre (g)
Daily allowance: 2 tubs Energen F-Plan Crunchy Bran Muesli, ½ pint (285ml) skimmed milk, two items of fruit	420	20

	Calories	Fibre (g)
Breakfast		

Breakfast
1 tub Energen F-Plan Crunchy Bran
Muesli with milk from allowance

1 large thin slice (1¼oz, 35g) wholemeal bread,
toasted and spread with ½oz (7g) low-fat spread
and 1 level teaspoon honey or marmalade · · · 115 · · · 3

Light meal
1 McCain Deep 'n' Delicious Cheese & Onion
or Cheese & Tomato Pizza
4oz (115g) canned baked beans in tomato
sauce

An orange from allowance · · · 270 · · · 9·5

Main meal
Mushroom omelet: 2 eggs (size 3), beaten
with 2 tablespoons water, salt and pepper
and a pinch of mixed herbs. Cook in ½oz
(7g) low-fat spread in a non-stick omelet pan
and fill with the contents of a 7½oz (213g)
can Chesswood Sliced Large Mushrooms in
Brine, drained
Half 7oz (198g) can Green Giant Mexicorn
Golden Corn

150g carton low-fat fruit-flavoured yogurt
with 7¾oz (220g) can Boots Shapers Pears
in Low-Calorie Syrup · · · 445 · · · 12·5

Any-time snacks
1 tub Energen F-Plan Crunchy Bran
Muesli with milk from allowance

An apple or pear from allowance

	Calories	Fibre (g)
TOTAL	1,250	45

1,500 CALORIE MENU 1

	Calories	Fibre (g)
Daily allowance: ½ pint (285ml) skimmed milk, two items of fruit	200	5
Breakfast 2oz (55g) Allinson Crunchy Bran with ½oz (15g) sultanas or raisins and milk from allowance	165	16·5
Light meal 7½oz (215g) canned spaghetti in tomato sauce, topped with 1 egg (size 3), poached		
1 Jordans Original Crunchy Bar, Honey & Coconut		
1 average-sized banana (6oz, 170g)	435	6·5
Main meal 10oz (284g) pack Birds Eye Mediterranean Stir-Fry Vegetables, fried and mixed with 7oz (200g) canned tuna in brine, drained and flaked		
An orange from allowance	530	6·5
Any-time snacks An apple or pear from allowance		
2 Energen F-Plan Diet Brancrisps, spread with Princes Beef or Fried Chicken Spread (1¼oz, 35g) pot, and topped with 1oz (30g) sweet pickle	170	3
TOTAL	1,500	37·5

1,500 CALORIE MENU   2

	Calories	Fibre (g)
Daily allowance: ½ pint (285ml) skimmed milk, two items of fruit	200	5

Breakfast
1½oz (45g) Kellogg's All-Bran with 1oz (30g) Whitworth's (no-need-to-soak) dried apricots, chopped, and milk from allowance — 150 — 18

Light meal
1 pot Golden Wonder Chicken & Mushroom Pot Noodle

An apple or pear from allowance — 380 — 8·5

Main meal
14oz (397g) tray Birds Eye Captain's Pie (cod in butter sauce topped with potato and a sprinkling of Cheddar cheese)
4oz (115g) frozen peas, boiled

8oz (227g) can Koo Peach Slices in Apple Juice
2oz (55g) portion vanilla ice-cream — 670 — 13

Any-time snack and drinks
An orange from allowance

2 bar measures of spirits (gin, rum, vodka or whisky) with low-calorie mixers *or*
1 glass (4fl oz, 115ml) sweet white wine *or*
other drinks chosen from chart (p. 285) to value of 100 calories — 100 — 0

| **TOTAL** | 1,500 | 44·5 |

1,500 CALORIE MENU   3

	Calories	Fibre (g)
Daily allowance: ½ pint (285ml) skimmed milk, two items of fruit	200	5

Breakfast
2oz (55g) Allinson Crunchy Bran with
½oz (15g) sultanas or raisins and milk from
allowance | 165 | 16·5

Light meal
15oz (425g) can Baxter's or Campbell's
Granny Lentil Soup
2 Energen F-Plan Diet Brancrisps

An apple or pear from allowance | 285 | 12·5

Main meal
Half 14·8oz (419g) tray frozen Marco &
Carlo Lasagne, cooked
Half 1lb 1oz (482g) can Green Giant
American Bean Salad

Half 8oz (227g) can Del Monte Pineapple
Slices in Natural Juice
150g carton Eden Vale Natural
Yogurt with Honey | 560 | 8

Any-time snacks and drinks
Drink(s) from chart (p. 285) to value of
160 calories

1 small (25g) packet potato crisps, any
flavour

An orange from allowance | 290 | 3

| TOTAL | 1,500 | 45 |

1,500 CALORIE MENU   4

	Calories	Fibre (g)
Daily allowance: ½ pint (285ml) skimmed milk, two items of fruit	200	5

Breakfast
1½oz (45g) Kellogg's All-Bran with 1oz (30g) Whitworth's (no-need-to-soak) dried apricots, chopped, and milk from allowance — **150** — **18**

Light meal
Crab and salad sandwich: 2 large thin slices (1¼oz, 35g each) wholemeal bread filled with contents of 1½oz (42g) can John West Dressed Crab, 1 tablespoon low-calorie salad dressing, 1 lettuce leaf, 1 tomato, sliced, a few slices of cucumber, a few sprigs of watercress

1 Prewett's Fruit & Nut Dessert Bar

An orange from allowance — **380** — **11**

Main meal
1 individual Birds Eye Frozen Chicken & Mushroom Pie, cooked
8oz (225g) Birds Eye frozen Cauliflower, Peas & Carrots

2oz (55g) vanilla ice-cream with an average-sized banana (6oz, 170g), sliced — **605** — **15**

Any-time snacks
An apple or pear from allowance

1 Cadbury's Crunchie, large *or* Rowntree Mackintosh Walnut Whip, Plain Chocolate

	Calories	Fibre (g)
Vanilla *or* St Michael Milk Chocolate Wafer Bar (30g)	165	0

	Calories	Fibre (g)
TOTAL	1,500	49

1,500 CALORIE MENU 5

	Calories	Fibre (g)
Daily allowance: ½ pint (285ml) skimmed milk, two items of fruit	200	5

Breakfast

	Calories	Fibre (g)
2oz (55g) Allinson Crunchy Bran with ½oz (15g) sultanas or raisins and milk from allowance	165	16·5

Light meal
8oz (225g) canned baked beans in tomato sauce
2oz (55g) frozen beefburger, grilled

	Calories	Fibre (g)
An orange from allowance	290	16·5

Main meal
1 Bowyer's individual (5oz, 142g) pork pie
Mixed salad: 1 average-sized tomato, sliced, a few spring onions, 1oz (30g) cucumber, sliced, a few sprigs of watercress, a few lettuce leaves, 1oz (30g) green pepper, sliced, and 1 tablespoon oil-free French dressing

	Calories	Fibre (g)
150g carton low-fat fruit-flavoured yogurt	705	4

	Calories	Fibre (g)
Any-time snacks and drinks An apple or pear from allowance		
1 Energen F-Plan Diet Brancrisp, spread with 1 triangle cheese spread and topped with a few sprigs of watercress or slices of cucumber		
1 drink chosen from chart (p. 285) to the value of 75 calories	140	2·5
TOTAL	1,500	44·5

1,500 CALORIE MENU   6

	Calories	Fibre (g)
Daily allowance: ½ pint (285ml) skimmed milk, two items of fruit	200	5
Breakfast 1½oz (45g) Kellogg's All-Bran with 1oz (30g) Whitworth's (no-need-to-soak) dried apricots, chopped, and milk from allowance	150	18
Light meal Chicken and ham with tomato sandwich: 2 large thin slices (1½oz, 35g each) wholemeal bread, filled with Shippams Chicken & Ham Paste, 1·23oz (35g) pot, and 1 large tomato, sliced 1 small packet (25g) potato crisps, any flavour		
An apple or pear from allowance	360	10

	Calories	Fibre (g)
Main meal		
1 pack Birds Eye Braised Kidneys in Gravy		
Half medium packet Smash Potato Pieces, made up without butter		
4oz (115g) frozen mixed vegetables (Birds Eye or Ross)		
1 individual Birds Eye Trifle or Super Mousse	500	10·5
Any-time snacks and drinks		
An orange from allowance		
1 Quaker Harvest Crunch Bar, almond or peanut		
Drinks chosen from chart (p. 285) to the value of 200 calories	290	1
TOTAL	1,500	44·5

F-PLAN FOR MEN

Although most men could achieve a very successful weight loss on any of the 1,500 calorie menus in this book, these menus have been especially designed to take into account their different lifestyles. The menus which total between 1,200 and 1,300 calories are intended for the drinking man, allowing him to 'spend' between 200 and 300 calories (to bring the daily total up to 1,500 calories) on alcoholic drinks (see chart, p. 285). Those menus with meals eaten in a restaurant, etc., have an *approximate* calorie and fibre total, since it is impossible to calculate the value of such meals accurately.

Varied eating habits have been taken into account in these menus. Although breakfasts have been included each day, if you are a non-breakfast eater you can keep this meal until later in the day. Various types of lunches – for example, packed lunches, café, restaurant, business, pub and Sunday/weekend lunches – have been included to cater for different needs. Some of the evening meals are easy-cook meals which might better suit the bachelor; others are suitable for the married man who eats his meals with his family. The recipes are all planned to serve one person, but the recipe ingredients can easily be multiplied by the number of people eating together, when appropriate.

Some variation from the basic F-Plan rules will be found in the 'daily allowances', since some men lack the time to make Fibre-Filler and others find skimmed milk unacceptable. In case anyone should be tempted to give up the diet for either of these reasons, half the menus do not include Fibre-Filler and a few menus include whole milk (in place of skimmed milk) in the daily allowance.

SPECIAL DIET NOTES

1. Decide whether or not you wish to include one or two alcoholic drinks in your daily menus.

2. On the days when you can do without alcohol, choose your menus from the 1,500 calorie daily menus.

3. Choose your menus from the 1,200–1,300 calorie menus on days when you know you will want an alcoholic drink, and decide which drinks you will have using the chart (p. 285).

4. Make sure that you 'spend' only an additional 200–300 calories on drinks if you want to achieve a good weight loss.

5. Select menus for at least two or three days, preferably one week at a time, so that you can plan to have the right foods ready at the right time.

6. Don't just choose one menu and repeat it every day. Use a variety of menus which will ensure a variety of foods and hence a variety of nutrients, which is essential for good health.

7. The 'daily allowance' of essential basic F-Plan diet foods varies throughout the menus, so ensure that you know what is included in the 'daily allowance' of each menu you select.

8. Non-alcoholic drinks, such as sugarless tea and coffee, either black or with skimmed or whole milk from the daily allowance, low-calorie labelled bottled and canned drinks, and water can be drunk in unlimited amounts at any time of the day.

1,500 CALORIE MENU 1
(no additional alcohol)

	Calories	Fibre (g)
Daily allowance: Fibre-Filler (p. 24), ½ pint (285ml) skimmed milk, an orange and an apple or pear	400	20

Breakfast
Whole daily portion of Fibre-Filler with milk from allowance

	Calories	Fibre (g)

Lunch (to carry to work)
* Ham Double-Decker Sandwich

1 small packet (25g) potato crisps, any
flavour

An apple or pear from allowance — 445 — 13·5

Evening meal
8oz (225g) chicken leg joint, grilled or oven
baked without added fat
7oz (200g) potato, baked in its jacket (see
p. 31 for cooking instructions), served
with ½oz (15g) low-fat spread
4oz (115g) Brussels sprouts, boiled
4oz (115g) carrots, boiled

2oz (55g) vanilla ice-cream with 2 wafers
An orange from allowance — 655 — 11·5

TOTAL	1,500	45

* Ham Double-Decker Sandwich

Serves 1

3 large thin slices (1¼oz, 35g each) wholemeal bread
a little made mustard
1oz (30g) sliced boiled lean ham
¼ carton mustard and cress
½oz (7g) low-fat spread
1 medium tomato, sliced
a few slices of cucumber
a few lettuce leaves
salt and pepper

Spread one slice of the bread with a little made mustard, top with the slice of boiled ham and the mustard and cress. Spread the second slice of bread lightly with half the low-fat spread and place spread side up on the ham. Cover with slices of tomato, cucumber and lettuce leaves. Season to taste. Spread the third slice of bread with the remaining low-fat spread and place spread side down on top of the sandwich. Cut into four small sandwiches and pack.

1,500 CALORIE MENU   2
(no additional alcohol)

	Calories	Fibre (g)
Daily allowance: Fibre-Filler (p. 24), ½ pint (285ml) silver-top (whole pasteurized) milk, an orange and an apple or pear	490	20
Breakfast Whole daily portion of Fibre-Filler with milk from allowance		
An orange from allowance		
Lunch (to carry to work) * Crunchy Cheese and Tomato Rolls		
2 fingers Kit Kat *or* 2 Hovis digestive biscuits		
An apple or pear from allowance	490	12
Evening meal 6oz (170g) cod, haddock or coley fillets, brushed with 1 teaspoon cooking oil and grilled (serve with a wedge of lemon) 4oz (115g) frozen peas, boiled		

	Calories	Fibre (g)
4oz (115g) canned tomatoes		
5oz (140g) boiled potatoes (no butter) *or* half medium-size packet Smash Potato Pieces, made up with boiling water (no butter)		
4oz (115g) canned pineapple slices in natural juice		
2oz (55g) portion vanilla ice-cream	520	12·5
TOTAL	1,500	44·5

* Crunchy Cheese and Tomato Rolls

Serves 1

2 wholemeal rolls, e.g. Allinson's (1½oz, 42g each)
1oz (30g) mature Cheddar cheese, grated
2 tablespoons low-calorie salad dressing
1 large stick celery, finely chopped
1 medium carrot, grated
2 medium tomatoes, sliced

Split the rolls. Mix the grated cheese with the salad dressing, finely chopped celery and grated carrot. Spread half the mixture over the cut surface of the bottom half of each roll. Cover each with sliced tomato and replace the top half of each roll. Pack.

1,500 CALORIE MENU 3
(no additional alcohol)

	Calories	Fibre (g)
Daily allowance: Fibre-Filler (p. 24), ½ pint (285ml) silver-top (whole pasteurized) milk, an orange and an apple or pear	490	20

	Calories	Fibre (g)
Breakfast		
Whole daily portion of Fibre-Filler with milk from allowance		
Lunch (to carry to work)		
2 * Sardine and Celery Sandwiches		
An apple or pear from allowance	575	15
Evening meal		
8oz (225g) individual frozen shepherd's pie		
4oz (115g) cabbage, boiled		
4oz (115g) carrots, boiled		
1 Ryvita crispbread, brown or original, with 1oz (30g) Edam, Brie, Camembert or processed cheese (no butter)		
2 sticks celery		
An orange from allowance	435	10·5
TOTAL	1,500	45·5

* Sardine and Celery Sandwiches

Serves 1

4 large thin slices (1¼oz, 35g each) wholemeal bread
½oz (15g) low-fat spread
4½oz (130g) canned sardines in tomato sauce
¼ teaspoon vinegar
2 large sticks celery, finely chopped
a few sprigs of watercress

Spread each of the slices of bread lightly with low-fat spread. Mash the sardines with the vinegar and mix with the chopped celery. Spread the sardine filling over two slices of bread. Cover with sprigs of watercress and top with the remaining slices of bread to make two rounds of sandwiches. Cut each sandwich into two or four pieces and pack.

1,500 CALORIE MENU
(no additional alcohol)

4

	Calories	Fibre (g)
Daily allowance: Fibre-Filler (p. 24), ½ pint (285ml) skimmed milk, an orange and an apple or pear	400	20

Breakfast
Whole daily portion of Fibre-Filler with milk from allowance

Business/restaurant lunch or evening meal
Slice (8oz, 225g) cantaloupe, honeydew or yellow melon (no sugar)
8oz (225g) steak, medium grilled
1 jacket baked potato, with a small pat of butter or a foil-wrapped portion of butter
Green or mixed salad without dressing

1 glass (4fl oz, 115ml) dry red wine	approx. 890	8

Light meal
15·3oz (435g) can Heinz Vegetable & Lentil Big Soup

An orange and an apple or pear from allowance	210	9

TOTAL	approx. 1,500	37

1,500 CALORIE MENU
(no additional alcohol)

5

	Calories	Fibre (g)
Daily allowance: Fibre-Filler (p. 24), ½ pint (285ml) skimmed milk, an orange and an apple or pear	400	20

	Calories	Fibre (g)

Breakfast
Whole daily portion of Fibre-Filler with
milk from allowance

Café/restaurant lunch
Mushroom omelet and chips

An apple or pear from allowance
(*Note*. If fresh fruit is not served in the café
or restaurant omit the dessert and eat the
fruit at home later in the day.)   approx. 600   3·5

Evening meal
* Kidney Bean, Cauliflower and Corned
Beef Salad

2 Ryvita crispbreads, brown or original,
with 1oz (30g) Edam, Brie, Camembert or
processed cheese (no butter)
2 sticks celery

An orange from allowance   500   18·5

TOTAL	approx. 1,500	42

* **Kidney Bean, Cauliflower and Corned Beef Salad**

Serves 1

4oz (115g) canned kidney beans, drained
4oz (115g) fresh cauliflower, broken into florets
2 or 3 spring onions, chopped *or* 1oz (30g) onion, sliced
3oz (85g) corned beef, diced
2oz (55g) green pepper, chopped

3 tablespoons oil-free French dressing
a pinch of curry powder
a few sprigs of watercress
2 small tomatoes, or 1 large one, cut in wedges

Put all the ingredients except the watercress and tomatoes into a bowl and toss until well mixed. Leave to stand for 30 minutes before serving. Serve garnished with sprigs of watercress and wedges of tomato.

1,500 CALORIE MENU   6
(no additional alcohol)

	Calories	Fibre (g)
Daily allowance: ¼ pint (285ml) skimmed milk, an orange and an apple or pear	200	5
Breakfast 1½oz (45g) All Bran or Bran Buds with ½oz (15g) sultanas and milk from daily allowance		
1 large thin slice (1¼oz, 35g) wholemeal bread, spread with ¼oz (7g) low-fat spread and 1 level teaspoon honey or marmalade	245	15
Lunch (to carry to work) * Prawn and Salad Double-Decker Sandwiches		
2 fingers Kit Kat or 2 Hovis digestive biscuits		
An apple or pear from allowance	460	10·5

	Calories	Fibre (g)

Evening meal

7oz (200g) raw weight pork chop, grilled,
with fat cut off before serving

1oz (30g) apple sauce
4cz (115g) button mushrooms, poached in
stock *or* 7½oz (215g) canned mushrooms in
brine
4oz (115g) frozen mixed peas, sweetcorn
and peppers, boiled
5oz (140g) boiled new potatoes *or* 7oz
(200g) canned new potatoes, drained (no
butter)

1 Ryvita crispbread (no butter)
½oz (15g) Edam, Brie, Camembert or
processed cheese
1 stick celery

An orange from allowance	595	16
TOTAL	1,500	46·5

---

* Prawn and Salad Double-Decker Sandwiches

Serves 1

3 large thin slices (1½oz, 35g each) wholemeal bread
2 tablespoons low-calorie salad dressing
2 oz (55g) peeled prawns (fresh, frozen or canned)
a few sprigs of watercress
1 medium tomato, sliced
a few slices of cucumber

Spread all three slices of bread on one side with a little of the low-calorie salad dressing. Mix the prawns with the remaining salad dressing and use to cover one slice of the bread. Place second slice of bread on top of the prawns and cover with the watercress, tomato and cucumber. Place the final slice of bread, spread side down, on top of the sandwich. Cut into four small sandwiches and pack.

1,500 CALORIE MENU 7
(no additional alcohol)

	Calories	Fibre (g)
Daily allowance: ½ pint (285ml) skimmed milk, an orange and an apple or pear	200	5
Breakfast 2oz (55g) Prewett's Bran Muesli with milk from allowance An average-sized banana (6oz, 170g)	255	16
Lunch (to carry to work) Cheese and pickle bap: 2oz (55g) wholemeal bap (round flat roll), split and filled with 1oz (30g) piccalilli, chopped finely and mixed with 1oz (30g) Cheddar cheese, grated 3oz (85g) carrots, cut into sticks 1 large stick celery, cut into short sticks 1 small packet (25g) potato crisps, any flavour An orange from allowance	400	12
Evening meal * Bacon and Liver Casserole 7oz (200g) baked jacket potato (baked in the oven with the casserole, see p. 31) 4oz (115g) canned tomatoes 4oz (115g) frozen peas, boiled An apple or pear from allowance	645	16
TOTAL	1,500	49

* Bacon and Liver Casserole

Serves 1

4oz (115g) pig's liver
1 level tablespoon cornflour
a generous pinch of dried mixed herbs
salt and pepper
2 rashers streaky bacon, rind removed
1 small (about 2oz, 55g) onion, sliced
¼ beef stock cube

Set the oven to 180°C (350°F, gas 4). Slice the liver. Mix the cornflour with the mixed herbs and a little salt and pepper. Toss the liver in the mixture. Cut each of the bacon rashers into three pieces. Arrange half the bacon pieces on the bottom of an ovenproof dish. Cover with half the onion slices, the liver, the rest of the onion slices and finally the remaining bacon pieces. Dissolve the stock cube in 6 tablespoons boiling water and pour over the ingredients in the dish. Cover with a tightly fitting lid or foil and cook in the oven for 1 hour.

1,500 CALORIE MENU 8
(no additional alcohol)

	Calories	Fibre (g)
Daily allowance: ½ pint (285ml) skimmed milk, an orange and an apple or pear	200	5
Breakfast 1½oz (45g) Allinson Crunchy Bran with 1oz (30g) dried apricots, chopped, and milk from allowance	145	22
Restaurant/café lunch Spaghetti bolognese		
Ice-cream	approx. 575	1·5

	Calories	Fibre (g)

Evening meal
* Fish bake
5oz (140g) boiled potatoes, mashed
without butter, or half medium packet
Smash Potato Pieces, made up with boiling
water (no butter)
4oz (115g) frozen peas, boiled

1 Ryvita crispbread, brown or original, no
butter
1oz (30g) Edam, Brie, Camembert or
processed cheese
2 sticks celery

An orange and an apple or pear from
allowance

	Calories	Fibre (g)
An orange and an apple or pear from allowance	580	14
TOTAL	approx. 1,500	42·5

* Fish Bake

Serves 1

two 4oz (115g) frozen cod, coley or haddock steaks, thawed
4·9oz (140g) can Campbell's Condensed Cream of Mushroom
   Soup
1 tablespoon skimmed milk from allowance
1 tablespoon finely chopped onion

Place the two thawed fish steaks in the bottom of a small ovenproof
dish. Put the soup into a pan, add the milk and chopped onion and
heat gently, stirring, until the soup is near boiling point. Pour over
the fish steaks and bake at 190°C (375°F, gas 5), for 30 minutes.
Serve hot.

1,500 CALORIE MENU 9
(no additional alcohol)

	Calories	Fibre (g)
Daily allowance: ½ pint (285ml) silver-top (whole pasteurized) milk, an orange and an apple or pear	290	5
Breakfast 1½oz (45g) All Bran or Bran Buds with ½oz (15g) sultanas and milk from allowance		
An orange from allowance	150	12
Lunch (to take to work) * Tuna and Sweetcorn Rolls 3oz (85g) carrots, cut into sticks 1 medium tomato, cut into wedges		
1 Jordans Original Crunchy Bar, Honey & Coconut		
An apple or pear from allowance	500	13
Evening meal 14·8oz (419g) pack frozen Marco & Carlo Lasagne (whole pack, not half pack as suggested on the packet) 5oz (140g) frozen mixed cauliflower, peas and carrots, boiled		
An average-sized banana (6oz, 170g)	560	11
TOTAL	1,500	41

* Tuna and Sweetcorn Rolls

Serves 1

2 Allinson wholemeal snack rolls (1½oz, 42g each)
3½oz (100g) canned tuna in brine, drained

1oz (30g) Bicks Corn Relish
a few slices of cucumber

Split the bread rolls in half. Flake the tuna and mix with the corn relish. Spread the tuna mixture on the bottom half of each roll, cover with sliced cucumber and top with the remaining half of roll. Pack.

1,500 CALORIE MENU   10
(no additional alcohol)

	Calories	Fibre (g)
Daily allowance: ½ pint (285ml) silver-top (whole pasteurized) milk, an orange and an apple or pear	290	5
Breakfast 2oz (55g) Prewett's Bran Muesli with milk from allowance	175	12·5
Sunday lunch 3oz (85g) lean roast sirloin beef 2fl oz (55ml) thin fat-free gravy 4oz (115g) Brussels sprouts, boiled 4oz (115g) roast potato 4oz (115g) carrots, boiled		
* Banana Melba	610	16
Evening meal 1 McCain Deep 'n' Delicious Ham & Mushroom Pizza * Coleslaw		
2 Hovis digestive biscuits		
An orange and an apple or pear from allowance	425	9·5
TOTAL	1,500	43

* Banana Melba

Serves 1

2oz (55g) portion vanilla ice-cream
6oz (170g) banana
2oz (55g) fresh or frozen raspberries
1 rounded teaspoon icing sugar

Arrange the ice-cream on an oval flat dish. Peel the banana, cut it
in half and arrange the two halves on either side of the ice-cream.
Crush or liquidize the raspberries with the icing sugar and spoon
over the ice-cream. Serve at once.

* Coleslaw

Serves 1

4oz (115g) white cabbage, shredded
2oz (55g) carrot, grated
1oz (30g) onion, finely chopped
1 large stick celery, finely chopped
2 walnut halves, chopped
2 tablespoons low-calorie salad dressing

Mix all the ingredients together in a bowl thoroughly.

FOR THE DRINKING MAN   1
1,200–1,300 Calorie menu

	Calories	Fibre (g)
Daily allowance: Fibre-Filler (p. 24), ½ pint (285ml) skimmed milk, an orange and an apple or pear	400	20

Breakfast
Whole daily portion of Fibre-Filler with
milk from allowance

	Calories	Fibre (g)
Lunch (to carry to work)		
* Liver Sausage and Beetroot Double-Decker Sandwich		
2 Hovis digestive biscuits		
An apple or pear from allowance	465	11·5
Evening meal		
* Continental Tuna Stir-fry		
An orange from allowance	360	6·5
TOTAL	**1,225**	**38**

* Liver Sausage and Beetroot Double-Decker Sandwich

Serves 1

3 large thin slices (1¼oz, 35g each) wholemeal bread
1oz (30g) thinly sliced liver sausage
¼ carton mustard and cress
¼oz (7g) low-fat spread
1oz (30g) sliced pickled beetroot
2 lettuce leaves, shredded

Cover the first slice of bread with sliced liver sausage and mustard and cress. Top with the second slice of bread. Spread the upper surface of the second slice of bread with low-fat spread and one side of the third slice of bread. Cover the second slice of bread with sliced beetroot and shredded lettuce. Place the third slice of bread spread side down, on top. Cut into four sandwiches. Pack.

* Continental Tuna Stir-Fry

Serves 1

10oz (284g) pack Birds Eye Continental Stir-Fry Vegetables
3½oz (100g) canned tuna in brine, drained

Cook the stir-fry vegetables according to pack instructions. Flake the tuna and stir into the vegetables and heat through. Turn out on to a warm serving dish and serve at once.

FOR THE DRINKING MAN   2
1,200–1,300 Calorie menu

	Calories	Fibre (g)
Daily allowance: Fibre-Filler (p. 24), ½ pint (285ml) skimmed milk, an orange and an apple or pear	400	20
Breakfast Whole daily portion of Fibre-Filler with milk from allowance		
An average-sized banana (6oz, 170g)	80	3·5
Lunch (to carry to work) * 2 Cottage Cheese and Celery Sandwiches		
An apple or pear from allowance	420	13
Evening meal 13·6oz (385g) pack Marco & Carlo Spaghetti Bolognese (whole pack, not half as pack suggests) Cucumber, tomato and celery salad: 2oz (55g) cucumber, sliced, with 2 medium tomatoes, sliced, and 1 large stick celery, diced and sprinkled with 1 tablespoon oil-free French dressing and a few chopped chives (optional)		
An orange from allowance	350	3
TOTAL	1,250	36

* Cottage Cheese and Celery Sandwiches

Serves 1

4oz (115g) cottage cheese (natural, with chives or with onions
  and peppers)
1 large stick celery, finely chopped
salt and pepper
4 large thin slices (1½oz, 35g each) wholemeal bread
½ carton mustard and cress

Mix the cottage cheese with the chopped celery and salt and pepper
to taste. Fill two of the slices of bread with half of the cottage
cheese mixture and half the mustard and cress. Repeat with the
second two slices of bread to make two rounds of sandwiches. Cut
into smaller sandwiches; pack.

FOR THE DRINKING MAN   3
1,200–1,300 Calorie menu

	Calories	Fibre (g)
Daily allowance: Fibre-Filler (p. 24), ½ pint (285ml) skimmed milk, an orange and an apple or pear	400	20
Breakfast Whole daily portion of Fibre-Filler with milk from allowance 1 Ryvita crispbread, brown or original, spread with ¼oz (7g) low-fat spread and 1 teaspoon honey	65	1
Business/restaurant lunch or evening meal 8oz (225g) steak, medium grilled Green or mixed salad without dressing		
Fresh fruit salad without cream	approx. 520	7

	Calories	Fibre (g)

Drinks extra (see chart, p. 285)

Light meal
Baked beans and egg on toast: 2 large
thin slices (1½oz, 35g each) wholemeal
bread, toasted, 8oz (225g) canned baked
beans in tomato sauce and 1 egg (size 3),
poached

An orange and an apple or pear from allowance	290	14

TOTAL	approx. 1,275	42

FOR THE DRINKING MAN   4
1,200–1,300 Calorie menu

	Calories	Fibre (g)
Daily allowance: Fibre-Filler (p. 24), ½ pint (285ml) skimmed milk, an orange and an apple or pear	400	20

Breakfast
Whole daily portion of Fibre-Filler with
milk from allowance

Pub or sandwich bar lunch
1 round of ham sandwiches (made from 2
large slices of bread, lightly buttered and
filled with ham)

1 small packet (25g) potato crisps, any flavour	approx. 515	5

Drinks extra (see chart, p. 285)

	Calories	Fibre (g)
Evening meal		
* Chicken Salad		
* Prune Compôte	335	16·5

TOTAL	approx. 1,250	41·5

* Chicken Salad

Serves 1

3oz (85g) cooked chicken
4oz (115g) red or white cabbage, shredded
1 tablespoon finely chopped onion
1 dessert apple from allowance, cored and chopped
2 teaspoons lemon juice
2 tablespoons oil-free French dressing
salt and pepper
a few chicory or lettuce leaves
a few sprigs of watercress
a few slices of cucumber

Remove any skin from the chicken and slice. Put the cabbage, onion and apple into a bowl. Add the lemon juice and oil-free French dressing and mix all together well. Season to taste with salt and pepper. Arrange the cabbage salad on a serving dish with the sliced chicken, chicory or lettuce leaves, sprigs of watercress and slices of cucumber.

* Prune Compôte

Serves 1

2oz (55g) dried prunes
4 drops angostura bitters (optional)
a strip of lemon peel
1 level teaspoon sugar
1 orange from allowance, segmented
1 small (5½oz, 155g) banana, peeled and sliced

Cover the prunes with cold water and leave to stand overnight. Place the prunes and liquid in a pan and add the angostura bitters, if used, and lemon peel. Cover with a lid and simmer for 20 minutes. Remove the lemon peel and stir in the sugar. If serving hot, add the orange segments and sliced banana, heat through and serve. If serving cold, allow the prunes to cool before adding the orange segments and sliced banana.

FOR THE DRINKING MAN   5
1,200–1,300 Calorie menu

	Calories	Fibre (g)
Daily allowance: Fibre-Filler (p. 24), ½ pint (285ml) skimmed milk, an orange and an apple or pear	400	20
Breakfast Whole daily portion of Fibre-Filler with milk from allowance		
Lunch (to carry to work or eat at home) 10·6oz (300g) can Heinz Lentil Soup (heat and carry to work in a flask)		
2 Ryvita crispbreads, brown or original, spread with Marmite or yeast extract 1oz (30g) Cheddar cheese		
An apple or pear from allowance	350	8
Evening meal * Mixed Vegetable Curry with Rice		
An orange from allowance	470	19
TOTAL	1,220	47

* Mixed Vegetable Curry with Rice

Serves 1

2oz (55g) brown rice
½oz (15g) low-fat spread
1 small onion, chopped
½ small cooking apple, peeled, cored and chopped
1–2 level teaspoons curry powder
1 level teaspoon plain flour
¼ pint (140ml) vegetable stock or water
1 level teaspoon tomato purée
1 teaspoon lemon juice
4oz (115g) canned red kidney beans
4oz (115g) frozen mixed cauliflower, peas and carrots, thawed
1oz (30g) mushrooms, sliced
salt and pepper

Boil the rice in lightly salted water for about 25 minutes or until tender. While the rice is cooking, melt the low-fat spread in a saucepan. Add the onion and apple and cook gently for 5 minutes. Stir in the curry powder and flour and cook for 2 minutes, stirring all the time. Add the water or stock, bring to the boil, stirring, then add the tomato purée and lemon juice. Cover and simmer for 5 minutes. Add the drained kidney beans, mixed vegetables and mushrooms. Bring to the boil, cover and simmer gently for 15 minutes. Season to taste with salt and pepper. Drain the rice and serve with the vegetable curry.

FOR THE DRINKING MAN 6
1,200–1,300 Calorie menu

	Calories	Fibre (g)
Daily allowance: ½ pint (285ml) skimmed milk, an orange and an apple or pear	200	5
Breakfast 1½oz (45g) Allinson Crunchy Bran with 1oz (30g) dried apricots, chopped, and milk from allowance	145	22

	Calories	Fibre (g)
Restaurant/café lunch		
Tomato soup (or any other soup you wish)		
Chicken salad (no sala ddressing)	approx. 385	3
Evening meal		
* Cheese and Spinach Omelet		
4oz (115g) canned baked beans in tomato sauce		
* Fruit Salad	520	17
TOTAL	approx. 1,250	47

* Cheese and Spinach Omelet

Serves 1

3 eggs (size 3)
half 10·6oz (300g) pack frozen cut-leaf spinach, thawed
salt and pepper
½oz (7g) low-fat spread
1oz (30g) Cheddar cheese, grated

Lightly beat the eggs with 2 tablespoons water. Stir in the thawed spinach and salt and pepper. Grease a non-stick omelet pan or small frying pan with the low-fat spread and heat the pan. Pour in the egg and spinach mixture and heat until set. Sprinkle the grated cheese over the omelet and continue to heat for 1 minute. Fold the omelet in half and turn out on to a warm plate. Serve at once.

* Fruit Salad

Serves 1

1 orange from allowance, segmented
1 apple or pear from allowance, cored and diced or sliced
2oz (55g) black grapes, halved and pips removed
3fl oz (85ml) low-calorie ginger ale

¼oz (7g) flaked almonds

Mix the orange segments, diced or sliced apple or pear and grapes with the low-calorie ginger ale. Sprinkle over the flaked almonds and serve immediately.

FOR THE DRINKING MAN   7
1,200–1,300 Calorie menu

	Calories	Fibre (g)
Daily allowance: ½ pint (285ml) skimmed milk, an orange and an apple or pear	200	5
Breakfast 2oz (55g) Boots Second Nature Bran & Oat Crunch with milk from allowance	205	11
Lunch (to carry to work) Peanut butter and watercress sandwich: 2 large thin slices (1¼oz, 35g each) wholemeal bread, filled with ½oz (15g) peanut butter and sprigs of watercress		
2oz (55g) carrot, cut into sticks 1 large stick celery, cut into short sticks		
An apple or pear from allowance	260	10·5
Evening meal * Beef in Red Wine Sauce 6oz (170g) broccoli or Brussels sprouts, boiled		
1 Energen F-Plan Diet Brancrisp, spread with 1 triangle (½oz, 15g) cheese spread		
An orange from allowance	585	16
TOTAL	1,250	42·5

* Beef in Red Wine Sauce

Serves 1

4oz (115g) lean braising steak
7·9oz (225g) can Batchelors Cannellini Beans, drained
Half 13½oz (375g) can Homepride Red Wine Cook-in-Sauce

Arrange the piece of braising steak, either whole or in bite-sized pieces, in the bottom of a small ovenproof dish. Tip the beans over the steak. Spoon over the wine sauce. Cover with a lid or foil and bake in the oven at 180°C (350°F, gas 4) for 1½ hours.

FOR THE DRINKING MAN 8
1,200–1,300 Calorie menu

	Calories	Fibre (g)
Daily allowance: ½ pint (285ml) skimmed milk, an orange and an apple or pear	200	5
Breakfast 1½oz (45g) All Bran or Bran Buds with an average-sized banana (6oz, 170g), sliced and with milk from allowance	185	15·5
Lunch (to take to work) Beefburger with bun: split a 2oz (55g) wholemeal bap and spread the cut surfaces with 1 rounded tablespoon sweet pickle. Fill with a grilled beefburger, standard size (cold beefburgers are as tasty as hot ones)		
1 tomato 1 large stick celery, cut into short sticks		
An orange from allowance	315	7·5

	Calories	Fibre (g)

Evening meal
5oz (140g) lamb chump chop, well grilled
2 teaspoons mint sauce
7½oz (215g) canned butter beans, heated
4 oz (115g) canned tomatoes, heated
5oz (140g) boiled potatoes (no butter)
or half medium packet Smash Potato
Pieces, made up with boiling water (no
butter)

An apple or pear from allowance

1 Hovis digestive biscuit	600	10

TOTAL	1,300	38

FOR THE DRINKING MAN: 9
1,200–1,300 Calorie Menu

	Calories	Fibre (g)
Daily allowance: ½ pint (285ml) silver-top (whole pasteurized) milk, an orange and an apple or pear	290	5

Breakfast
2oz (55g) Allinson Crunchy Bran with milk from allowance	130	15·5

Restaurant/café lunch
Grilled Dover sole
Mixed salad without dressing

Fruit sorbet	approx. 620	2

	Calories	Fibre (g)
Evening meal		
Baked beans on toast: 1 large thin slice (1¼oz, 35g) wholemeal bread, toasted, spread with ¼oz (7g) low-fat spread and topped with 8oz (225g) canned baked beans in tomato sauce, heated		
An orange and an apple or pear from allowance	260	19·5
TOTAL	approx. 1,300	42

FOR THE DRINKING MAN   10
1,200–1,300 Calorie menu

	Calories	Fibre (g)
Daily allowance: ½ pint (285ml) silver-top (whole pasteurized) milk, an orange and an apple or pear	290	5
Breakfast		
1½oz (45g) All Bran or Bran Buds with ½oz (15g) sultanas or raisins and milk from allowance	150	12

Sunday/weekend lunch
3oz (85g) portion roast chicken (meat only, with skin removed)
7oz (200g) jacket baked potato (for baking instructions see p. 31), served with ¼oz (7g) low-fat spread
3½oz (100g) canned sweetcorn
2oz (55g) button mushrooms poached in stock or seasoned water

8oz (225g) canned pear halves in apple juice

	Calories	Fibre (g)
1oz (30g, one small scoop) ice-cream or 1½ tablespoons single cream or half 150g carton low-fat natural yogurt	555	16

Evening meal
* Egg Salad
1 large thin slice (1¼oz, 35g) wholemeal bread spread with ¼oz (7g) low-fat spread

An orange and an apple or pear from allowance	255	6·5

TOTAL	1,250	39·5

* Egg Salad

Serves 1

1 egg (size 3), hard-boiled
2oz (55g) button mushrooms
1 tablespoon lemon juice
salt and pepper
a small bunch of watercress or a few lettuce leaves
1 tomato, sliced
2oz (55g) carrot, grated
1oz (30g) pickled beetroot, sliced or diced
1oz (30g) green pepper, sliced or 2oz (55g) cucumber, sliced
1 tablespoon low-calorie salad dressing

Shell and halve the egg. Slice the mushrooms and toss in the lemon juice. Season to taste with salt and pepper. Arrange a bed of watercress or lettuce on a plate, then arrange the halved egg, mushrooms, sliced tomato, grated carrot, sliced or diced beetroot and green pepper or cucumber on top. Pour the salad dressing over the egg.

F-PLAN FOR CHILDREN

Most children need hardly know they are on a diet when following these menus, since the F-Plan allows children to eat the foods they most like.

Although most slimming diets which allow a daily intake of 1,500 calories are quite safe for school-age children to follow, they are rarely produced with children in mind and hence they do not include their favourite foods.

A daily calorie allowance of 1,500 will achieve a good weight loss for most boys; the weight loss for girls (unless heavily over-weight) may be less spectacular. As long as there is no further weight gain or, better still, if there is a steady (even if fairly small) weight loss, then you will have a chance to 'grow into your weight'.

The following menus follow the basic F-Plan diet rules, and include those foods which my testers and junior informers tell me are most popular with children. All the daily menus provide 1,500 calories and between 35g and 50g of fibre.

The first ten menus include a daily portion of Fibre-Filler (p. 24) in the daily allowance; however, since some children do not like Fibre-Filler and would find a diet including it every day to be quite unacceptable, there are ten daily menus without Fibre-Filler. These all contain a bran-based breakfast cereal which partly replaces the Fibre-Filler. Also in the daily allowance, all twenty menus include two whole pieces of fruit (an orange and an apple or pear) and one pint (570ml) skimmed milk. The quantity of milk has been increased from the basic F-Plan diet allowance to ensure that children obtain adequate amounts of nutrients for their growth requirements.

SPECIAL DIET NOTES

1. Choose a week's menus at one time so that the food can be bought in advance.

2. Don't swap meals from one day's menu to another. Stick to the chosen menus – there should be sufficient to choose from for you to avoid foods which you particularly dislike. However, the same menu every day will not provide you with sufficient variety of foods and will be very boring. You do need to use several menus if you are dieting for more than a few days.

3. The skimmed milk allowance is used on your breakfast cereal or Fibre-Filler and where necessary in a bed-time drink or to make the custard or sauce called for in some of the menus. However, there should be enough skimmed milk for you to use it in tea as well. (Children should not drink coffee.) Although tea is not mentioned in the menus you are allowed to drink as many cups of tea each day as you like as long as you do not add sugar and use only skimmed milk from your allowance.

4. You can drink canned and bottled drinks labelled *low-calorie* and as much water as you like throughout the day.

5. The daily menus are divided up into breakfast, mid-morning snack, lunch, after-school snack, dinner and a bed-time drink or snack. However, if this arrangement of meals does not fit in with your life-style then you can rearrange the meals (e.g. eat the evening meal at lunchtime and keep the mid-morning snack until lunchtime or the evening) as long as at the end of the day you have only eaten those foods on the daily menu.

6. Some of the lunches are suitable for packing so that they can be eaten at school or on a picnic. Soups and salads can be packed as well as sandwiches – just remember to take the right tools along to eat them with.

7. The after-school snack becomes a teatime snack at weekends.

8. Finally, eat more slowly than you usually do. Foods high in fibre need more chewing than low-fibre foods so you will probably slow down anyway. Slow eating means that you have time to enjoy your food and should feel more satisfied at the end of a meal, whereas if you gobble your food down you forget all too quickly that you have eaten and want more food.

9. Remember that if you stick to your diet you will not only be fitter and healthier but life will be more fun.

1,500 CALORIE MENU   1
with Fibre-Filler

	Calories	Fibre (g)
Daily allowances: Fibre-Filler, 1 pint (570ml) skimmed milk, two items of fruit	500	20

Breakfast
Half portion of Fibre-Filler with milk from allowance

An orange from allowance

Mid-morning snack
1 Quaker Harvest Crunch Bar, peanut or almond — 90 — 1

Lunch
* Peanut Butter and Cucumber Sandwich

2oz (55g) carrot, cut into sticks

An apple or pear from allowance — 335 — 9·5

After-school snack
Remaining portion of Fibre-Filler with skimmed milk from allowance

Evening meal
2 frozen beefburgers, grilled
4oz (115g) canned baked beans in tomato sauce
4oz (115g) potatoes, boiled and mashed

2oz (55g) portion vanilla ice-cream with 2 wafers (optional) — 535 — 9

	Calories	Fibre (g)
Bed-time drink		
A cup of chocolate – 2 rounded teaspoons		
drinking chocolate with milk from		
allowance	40	0

TOTAL	1,500	39·5

* Peanut Butter and Cucumber Sandwich

2 large thin slices (1½oz, 35g each) wholemeal bread
1oz (30g) peanut butter
a few slices of cucumber

Spread both slices of the bread with the peanut butter and sandwich together with slices of cucumber.

1,500 CALORIE MENU
with Fibre-Filler   **2**

	Calories	Fibre (g)
Fibre-Filler, 1 pint (570ml) skimmed milk,		
two items of fruit	500	20
Breakfast		
Half portion of Fibre-Filler with milk from		
allowance		
1 large thin slice wholemeal bread,		
toasted and spread with ¼oz (7g) low-		
fat spread and Marmite or savoury yeast		
extract	110	3
Mid-morning snack		
1 Hovis digestive biscuit	55	0·5

	Calories	Fibre (g)
Lunch		
2 large pork sausages, grilled		
1 Ryvita crispbread, brown or original		
2 average-sized tomatoes		
1 large stick celery, cut into short lengths		
An apple or pear from allowance	315	3·5
After-school snack		
Remaining portion of Fibre-Filler with skimmed milk from allowance		
An orange from allowance		
Evening meal		
* Pasta with Meat Sauce		
1 average-sized banana (6oz, 170g)	480	12·5
Bed-time drink		
A cup of chocolate – 2 rounded teaspoons drinking chocolate with milk from allowance	40	0
TOTAL	1,500	39·5

* Pasta with Meat Sauce

Serves 1 (several portions of the meat sauce can be made up at one time and frozen until required)

2oz (55g) wholewheat pasta rings, shells or spaghetti

Meat sauce
4oz (115g) lean minced beef
1oz (30g) onion, peeled and finely chopped
1 stick celery, finely diced
¼ beef stock cube, dissolved in 5 tablespoons boiling water
salt and freshly ground pepper

a pinch of mixed herbs
1 teaspoon tomato purée
1oz (30g) canned baked beans in tomato sauce

Fry the minced beef in a non-stick saucepan until well browned. Drain off all the fat which has cooked out of the meat. Add the onion, celery and stock to the meat in the pan and bring to the boil, stirring. Reduce the heat, season to taste with salt and pepper and add the herbs and tomato purée. Cover and simmer gently for 30 minutes, stirring occasionally and adding more water if necessary to prevent the mixture boiling dry. Boil the pasta in salted water for about 12 minutes or until just tender. Drain and arrange on a plate. Stir the baked beans into the meat sauce and heat through for 2–3 minutes, then spoon over the pasta.

1,500 CALORIE MENU   3
with Fibre-Filler

	Calories	Fibre (g)
Daily allowances: Fibre-Filler, 1 pint (570ml) skimmed milk, two items of fruit	500	20
Breakfast Half portion of Fibre-Filler with milk from allowance 1 egg (size 3), boiled and served with 1 large thin slice wholemeal bread spread with a little Marmite or yeast extract	160	3
Mid-morning snack An apple or pear from allowance		
Lunch * Ham and Cheese Rolls * Corny Coleslaw 1 Ryvita crispbread, brown or original An orange from allowance	290	8

	Calories	Fibre (g)
After-school snack Remaining portion of Fibre-Filler with skimmed milk from allowance		
Evening meal 2 fish fingers, grilled without fat 3oz (85g) frozen peas, boiled 4oz (115g) oven chips, baked or grilled		
150g carton fruit-flavoured yogurt	510	9
Bed-time drink A cup of chocolate – 2 rounded teaspoons drinking chocolate with milk from allowance	40	0
TOTAL	**1,500**	**40**

* Ham and Cheese Rolls

Serves 1

2oz (55g) cottage cheese with pineapple
½ carton mustard and cress
2 thin slices (2oz, 55g) boiled lean ham

Mix the cottage cheese with the chopped mustard and cress. Divide equally between the two slices of ham and spread over the ham. Roll up the ham and secure with a cocktail stick if necessary.

* Corny Coleslaw

Serves 1

2oz (55g) firm white cabbage, shredded
2oz (55g) carrot, grated
2oz (55g) canned sweetcorn kernels, drained
1 tablespoon low-calorie salad dressing

Mix together the cabbage, carrot and sweetcorn. Then stir in the salad dressing.

1,500 CALORIE MENU   4
with Fibre-Filling

	Calories	Fibre (g)
Daily allowances: Fibre-Filler, 1 pint (570ml) skimmed milk, two items of fruit	500	20
Breakfast Half portion of Fibre-Filler with milk from allowance		
1 banana (7oz, 200g)	90	4
Mid-morning snack 1 Quaker Harvest Crunch Bar, peanut or almond	90	1
Lunch * 2 Cheese and Bean Snack Rolls 2oz (55g) raw carrot, cut into sticks An apple or pear from allowance	345	12·5
After-school snack 1 packet Allinson Wheateats	90	0·5
Evening meal 2 chicken drumsticks (3½oz, 100g each before cooking), grilled 2oz (55g) canned sweetcorn kernels 2oz (55g) mushrooms, poached in a little stock or seasoned water 2 average-sized tomatoes (4oz, 115g) A small bunch of watercress (1oz, 30g)		
Milk shake made from 1 sachet Kellogg's Two Shakes (any flavour) and ½ pint (285ml) skimmed milk from allowance	330	7

	Calories	Fibre (g)
Bed-time snack		
An orange from allowance		
1 Hovis digestive biscuit	55	0·5

TOTAL	1,500	45·5

* Cheese and Bean Snack Rolls

Serves 1

2 wholemeal snack rolls (1½oz, 45g each)
1oz (30g) mature Cheddar cheese, finely grated
2oz (55g) canned baked beans in tomato sauce
pepper to taste
a dash of Worcestershire sauce (optional)
½ carton mustard and cress

Split the rolls in half lengthwise. Mash the grated cheese and beans together using a fork. Season with pepper to taste and add the Worcestershire sauce if liked. Spread the cheese and bean mixture on the bottom half of each roll. Top with mustard and cress and the top half of each roll.

1,500 CALORIE MENU   5
with Fibre-Filler

	Calories	Fibre (g)
Daily allowances: Fibre-Filler, 1 pint (570ml) skimmed milk, two items of fruit	500	20
Breakfast		
Whole portion of Fibre-Filler with milk from allowance		
Mid-morning snack		
1 large thin slice wholemeal bread, toasted and spread with ½oz (7g) low-fat spread and 2 level teaspoons honey	130	3

	Calories	Fibre (g)
Lunch		
* Star Wars Soup		
2 Ryvita crispbreads, brown or original		
An apple or pear from allowance	380	19
After-school snack		
1 Hovis digestive biscuit	55	0·5
Evening meal		
Average-sized lamb loin chop (5oz, 140g raw weight), grilled		
1 tablespoon mint sauce		
4oz (115g) Brussels sprouts or cabbage, boiled		
4oz (115g) frozen mixed vegetables, boiled		
An orange from allowance	395	7·5
Bed-time drink		
A cup of chocolate – 2 rounded teaspoons drinking chocolate with skimmed milk from allowance	40	0
TOTAL	1,500	50

* Star Wars Soup

Serves 1

8oz (225g) canned baked beans in tomato sauce
2oz (55g) carrot, grated
1 beef stock cube
freshly ground pepper
2 pork chipolata sausages

Put the baked beans and grated carrot into a saucepan. Dissolve the stock cube in ¼ pint (140ml) boiling water and stir into the beans and carrot in the pan. Bring to the boil, cover and simmer gently for 15–20 minutes. Meanwhile, grill the chipolata sausages until well done, then cut each sausage into three equal pieces. Add to the soup, season to taste, and add a little boiling water if the soup is too thick. Serve hot with crispbreads.

1,500 CALORIE MENU 6
with Fibre-Filler

	Calories	Fibre (g)
Daily allowances: Fibre-Filler, 1 pint (570ml) skimmed milk, two items of fruit	500	20
Breakfast Half portion of Fibre-Filler with milk from allowance		
An orange from allowance		
Mid-morning snack 1 small packet (25g) potato crisps	130	3
Lunch * Sardine Sandwich		
150g carton fruit-flavoured low-fat natural yogurt	400	6
After-school snack An apple or pear from allowance		
Evening meal * Meaty Jacket Potato 1oz (30g) pickled beetroot 5oz (140g) fruit-flavoured jelly	470	6·5

	Calories	Fibre (g)

Bed-time snack
Half portion of Fibre-Filler with milk from
allowance

TOTAL	1,500	35·5

* Sardine Sandwich

Serves 1

2 sardines, canned in tomato sauce
1oz (30g) cottage cheese
salt and pepper
2 large thin slices (1¼oz, 35g each) wholemeal bread
2 lettuce leaves
a few slices of cucumber

Mash the sardines with the cottage cheese and season to taste. Fill
the two slices of bread with the sardine mixture, lettuce and
cucumber. Cut into four sandwiches.

* Meaty Jacket Potato

Serves 1

7oz (200g) potato
4oz (115g) raw minced beef
1oz (30g) chopped onion
1oz (30g) finely chopped celery
1 teaspoon tomato paste or purée
salt and pepper

Scrub the potato well, then bake by one of the methods described
on p. 31. Meanwhile, fry the minced breef in a saucepan without
added fat until well browned. Drain off and discard the fat. Add the
onion, celery, tomato paste or purée and 4–5 tablespoons water.
Heat until boiling, then simmer, covered, for 15 minutes. Cut the

baked jacket potato in half lengthwise, scoop out some of the flesh and mix with the hot minced beef mixture. Season to taste. Pile back into the jackets and serve.

1,500 CALORIE MENU 7
with Fibre-Filler

	Calories	Fibre (g)
Daily allowances: Fibre-Filler, 1 pint (570ml) skimmed milk, two items of fruit	500	20
Breakfast Half portion of Fibre-Filler with milk from allowance		
1 large thin slice wholemeal bread, toasted and spread with ½oz (7g) low-fat spread and Marmite or yeast extract	110	3
Mid-morning snack An apple or pear from allowance		
Lunch 1 Golden Wonder Chicken & Mushroom Pot Noodle *or* Spicy Curry Pot Noodle		
An orange from allowance	380	8·5/ 4·5
After-school snack Half portion Fibre-Filler with milk from allowance		
Evening meal * Hungarian Liver 4oz (115g) cabbage, boiled	450	11

	Calories	Fibre (g)
Bed-time drink		
Orange Milky: mix 1fl oz (30ml) low calorie		
orange squash with ¼ pint (140ml)		
skimmed milk from allowance		
1 Hovis digestive biscuit	60	0·5

TOTAL	**1,500**	**43/39**

*Hungarian Liver

Serves 1

4oz (115g) pig's liver
1 level tablespoon wholemeal flour
½oz (15g) low-fat spread
1 small onion, thinly sliced
2oz (55g) mushrooms, sliced
¼ pint (140ml) beef stock made from ⅓ stock cube
1 level teaspoon tomato purée
1½oz (45g) wholewheat macaroni
1 tablespoon natural yogurt
¼ teaspoon lemon juice

Cut the liver into thin slices horizontally and then vertically. Toss
in the wholemeal flour to coat. Heat the low-fat spread in a non-
stick pan and cook the onion over a low heat until soft. Add the
mushrooms and cook for a further 2–3 minutes. Add the liver
and cook for 3 minutes. Stir in the stock and tomato purée. Bring
to the boil, cover and simmer gently for 10 minutes. Meanwhile,
cook the macaroni in fast boiling, lightly salted water for 12–15
minutes, until just soft. Drain the macaroni well and arrange on
a serving plate. Spoon the liver mixture on top. Stir the yogurt
and lemon juice together and spoon on top of the liver and
pasta.

1,500 CALORIE MENU
8
with Fibre-Filler

	Calories	Fibre (g)
Daily allowances: Fibre-Filler, 1 pint (570ml) skimmed milk, two items of fruit	500	20
Breakfast Half portion of Fibre-Filler with milk from allowance		
2 rashers streaky bacon, well grilled and made into a sandwich with 1 large thin slice wholemeal bread spread with 1 teaspoon tomato ketchup or brown sauce	180	3
Mid-morning snack An apple or pear from allowance		
Lunch * Tuna Salad 1 Quaker Harvest Crunch Bar, peanut or almond	400	9·5
After-school snack Half portion of Fibre-Filler with milk from allowance		
Evening meal * One-Pan Supper 2oz (55g) vanilla ice-cream served with orange from allowance, cut into segments	380	4·5
Bed-time drink A cup of chocolate – 2 rounded teaspoons drinking chocolate with milk from allowance	40	0
TOTAL	1,500	37

* Tuna Salad

Serves 1

3½oz (100g) canned tuna in brine
1oz (30g) wholewheat pasta shells, cooked
3oz (85g) canned sweetcorn kernels with red and green pepper
1 stick celery, diced
2 level tablespoons low-fat natural yogurt
¼ teaspoon lemon juice
salt and pepper

Flake the tuna into a bowl. Add the pasta, sweetcorn and celery and mix well. Blend the yogurt with the lemon juice and add salt and pepper to taste. Add to the tuna mixture and toss gently until well mixed.

* One-Pan Supper

Serves 1

2 eggs (size 3)
salt and pepper
½oz (15g) low-fat spread
1oz (30g) chopped onion
1 small cooked potato (2oz, 55g), diced
1 average-sized fresh or canned tomato, chopped
1oz (30g) mushrooms, sliced
1oz (30g) cooked peas

Beat the eggs together with 2 tablespoons water and salt and pepper to taste. Melt the low-fat spread in a non-stick frying pan. Add the chopped onion, potato, tomato and mushrooms and cook over a gentle heat for 5 minutes, stirring frequently. Add the peas, then pour in the beaten egg. Cook over a moderate heat until the egg mixture is set on the bottom, then place under a hot grill to set the top and brown slightly. Turn out on to a warm plate and serve immediately.

1,500 CALORIE MENU 9
with Fibre-Filler

	Calories	Fibre (g)
Daily allowances: Fibre-Filler, 1 pint (570ml) skimmed milk, two items of fruit	500	20
Breakfast Half portion of Fibre-Filler with milk from allowance		
1 average-sized banana (6oz, 170g)	80	3·5
Mid-morning snack Kit Kat, 2 fingers	110	0
Lunch * Ploughman's Rolls 2 average-sized tomatoes a small bunch of watercress		
An apple or pear from allowance	330	8·5
After-school snack Remaining portion of Fibre-Filler with milk from allowance		
Evening meal * Quick Fish Pie		
5oz (140g) fruit-flavoured jelly with orange from allowance, cut into segments	475	9·5
Bed-time drink Orange Milky: 1fl oz (30ml) low-calorie orange squash with ¼ pint (140ml) skimmed milk from allowance	5	0
TOTAL	1,500	41·5

*Ploughman's Rolls

Serves 1

2 large thin slices wholemeal bread (1½oz, 35g each)
2 level tablespoons sweet pickle
2 pork chipolata sausages, well grilled

Flatten the two slices of bread by rolling with a rolling pin. Spread each slice with a tablespoon of sweet pickle. Place a chipolata sausage along one end of each slice of bread and roll the bread around the sausage. Secure with a cocktail stick if necessary.

* Quick Fish Pie

Serves 1

6oz (170g) packet frozen cod in cheese sauce
half medium packet Smash Potato Pieces
2oz (55g) frozen peas, boiled
½oz (15g) Cheddar cheese, grated

Cook the cod as directed on the packet. Make up the potato pieces with boiling water as directed. (*Note*. Do not add butter.) Pipe or spoon the potato around the edge of an individual flameproof dish. Place the peas in the bottom of the dish. Remove the fish and sauce from the bag and flake the fish into the sauce. Spoon over the peas. Top with the grated cheese and heat through under a hot grill until the cheese has melted and is lightly browned.

1,500 CALORIE MENU 10
with Fibre-Filler

	Calories	Fibre (g)
Daily allowances: Fibre-Filler, 1 pint (570ml) skimmed milk, two items of fruit	500	20

	Calories	Fibre (g)
Breakfast		
Half portion of Fibre-Filler with milk from allowance		
1 large thin slice wholemeal bread, toasted and spread with ½oz (7g) low-fat spread and 2 level teaspoons honey	130	3
Mid-morning snack		
An apple or pear from allowance		
Lunch		
* Vegetable and Lentil Soup		
2 Ryvita crispbreads, brown or original	225	10
After-school snack		
Kit Kat, 2 fingers		
An orange from allowance	110	0
Evening meal		
* Cheese Omelet		
5oz (140g) frozen grill chips, grilled		
2oz (55g) frozen peas, boiled	535	7·5
Bed-time snack		
Remaining portion of Fibre-Filler with milk from allowance		
TOTAL	1,500	42·5

* Vegetable and Lentil Soup

Serves 1 (several portions can be made up at one time and frozen in individual portions for future use)

1oz (30g) onion, sliced
2oz (55g) carrot, sliced

1 large stick celery, chopped
1½oz (45g) lentils
1 chicken or ham stock cube
salt and pepper

Put all the prepared vegetables in a pan with the lentils. Dissolve the stock cube in ¾ pint (425ml) boiling water. (*Note.* Vegetarians can omit the stock cube.) Add to the pan with salt and pepper to taste. Bring to the boil, cover and simmer gently for 1 hour.

* Cheese Omelet

Serves 1

2 eggs (size 3)
salt and pepper
¼oz (7g) low-fat spread
1oz (30g) Cheddar cheese, grated

Beat the eggs with 2 tablespoons water and seasoning to taste. Melt the low-fat spread in a non-stick omelet pan. Pour in the egg mixture and cook over a moderate heat until set. Sprinkle the cheese over the surface and allow to melt. Fold the omelet in half and turn out on to a warm plate. Serve at once.

1,500 CALORIE MENU
no Fibre-Filler

	Calories	Fibre (g)
Daily allowances: two items of fruit, 1 pint (570ml) skimmed milk	300	5
Breakfast 2oz (55g) Allinson Crunchy Bran with skimmed milk from allowance	130	15·5
Mid-morning snack An apple or pear from allowance		
1oz (30g) dried raisins	70	2

	Calories	Fibre (g)
Lunch		
* Pitta filled with corned beef, beetroot and cucumber		
An orange from allowance	350	3
After-school snack		
2 Ryvita crispbreads, brown or original, spread with 1 triangle cheese spread and topped with sliced cucumber or cress	95	2
Evening meal		
3½oz (100g) bacon steak, grilled without fat		
1 tablespoon brown sauce or tomato ketchup		
7oz (200g) potato, baked in its jacket (see p. 31)		
4oz (115g) canned baked beans in tomato sauce		
* Stewed Blackberries and Apple with Custard made with milk from allowance	505	14
Bed-time drink		
A cup of chocolate – 2 rounded teaspoons drinking chocolate with milk from allowance	40	0
TOTAL	1,500	41·5

* Pitta filled with Corned Beef, Beetroot and Cucumber

Serves 1

1 pitta (2oz, 55g)
2oz (55g) corned beef
1oz (30g) pickled beetroot, chopped
2oz (55g) cucumber, finely diced

Toast or bake the pitta until it puffs up to give a hollow centre. Cut the pitta in half. Mash the corned beef and mix with the chopped beetroot and cucumber. Fill the pitta with the corned beef mixture.

* Stewed Blackberries and Apple with Custard

Serves 1

2oz (55g) blackberries
4oz (115g) cooking apple, peeled, cored and sliced
3 level teaspoons granulated sugar
2 level teaspoons custard powder
4fl oz (115ml) skimmed milk from allowance

Stew the blackberries and apple with 2 tablespoons water in a covered pan until the fruit is tender. Stir in 1½ teaspoons of the sugar. Blend the custard powder and the remaining 1½ teaspoons of sugar with a little of the cold milk until smooth. Heat the remainder of the milk to boiling point in a small saucepan. Pour on to the blended custard powder, then return to the pan. Continue to heat, stirring continuously, until the custard has thickened. Serve with the fruit.

1,500 CALORIE MENU   2
no Fibre-Filler

	Calories	Fibre (g)
Daily allowances: two items of fruit, 1 pint (570ml) skimmed milk	300	5
Breakfast 2oz (55g) Kellogg's Sultana Bran with milk from allowance		
1 average-sized banana (6oz, 170g)	245	10·5
Mid-morning snack 2 Ryvita crispbreads, brown or original, each spread with 1 level tablespoon Waistline Low Calorie Vegetable Spread	80	2
Lunch * Welsh Soup with Wholemeal Croûtons		
An apple or pear from allowance	225	10

	Calories	Fibre (g)
After-school snack		
1 Jordans Original Crunchy Bar, Honey & Coconut	145	1
Evening meal		
* Egg and Beans with Cheese Crumble Topping		
2oz (55g) vanilla ice-cream served with orange from allowance, cut into segments	470	20·5
Bed-time snack and drink		
1 Ryvita crispbread spread with Marmite or yeast extract and topped with sliced cucumber		
Orange Milky: 1fl oz (30ml) low-calorie orange squash with ¼ pint (140ml) skimmed milk from allowance	35	1
TOTAL	1,500	50

* Welsh Soup with Wholemeal Croûtons

Serves 1 (several portions can be made up at one time and frozen in individual portions for future use)

5oz (140g) leeks, with coarse green leaves trimmed off
4oz (115g) peeled potato, thinly sliced or diced
½ chicken or vegetable stock cube
salt and pepper
1 large thin slice wholemeal bread (1¼oz, 35g)

Slice the leek thinly and place in a pan with the potato. Dissolve the stock cube in ½ pint (285 ml) boiling water and pour into the pan. Season to taste with salt and pepper. Bring to the boil, cover and simmer gently for 20 minutes. Purée the soup in a blender or food processor. Reheat, check seasoning and thin with water, if necessary. Toast the slice of wholemeal bread on both sides and cut into small cubes (croûtons). Serve the soup with the croûtons sprinkled on top.

* Egg and Beans with Cheese Crumble Topping

Serves 1

8oz (225g) canned baked beans in tomato sauce
1 egg (size 3)
2 average-sized tomatoes (2oz, 55g each), sliced
1oz (30g) wholemeal breadcrumbs
½oz (15g) Cheddar cheese, grated

Heat the beans and poach the egg. Spoon half the beans into a small ovenproof dish. Place the poached egg on top and then spoon over the remaining beans. Cover with the sliced tomatoes. Mix the breadcrumbs with the cheese and sprinkle over the top. Grill until crisp and bubbly.

1,500 CALORIE MENU **3**
no Fibre-Filler

	Calories	Fibre (g)
Daily allowances: two items of fruit, 1 pint (570ml) skimmed milk	300	5
Breakfast 1½oz (45g) Allinson Crunchy Bran with ½oz (15g) sultanas and milk from allowance	130	12·5
Mid-morning snack An apple or pear from allowance		
Lunch * Cheese with Nutty Coleslaw Orange from allowance	405	13

	Calories	Fibre (g)
After-school snack		
2 Hovis digestive biscuits	110	1·5
Evening meal		
1 frozen French bread pizza (any variety)		
Green salad: a few lettuce leaves, shredded,		
1oz (30g) sliced or diced cucumber,		
½ small green pepper, chopped, and a few		
sprigs of watercress		
4oz (115g) portion jelly		
1oz (30g) portion ice-cream	490	1·5
Bed-time snack		
1 Ryvita crispbread, brown or original,		
spread with 1 triangle cheese spread	65	1
TOTAL	1,500	34·5

* Cheese with Nutty Coleslaw

Serves 1

4oz (115g) firm white cabbage, shredded
2oz (55g) carrot, grated
2oz (55g) cooked peas
2oz (55g) canned sweetcorn kernels
1oz (30g) walnut pieces, roughly chopped
2 level tablespoons low-calorie salad dressing
1oz (30g) Edam cheese, grated

Mix the prepared vegetables and nuts together in a bowl. Stir in
the salad dressing. Arrange the coleslaw on a plate and pile the
grated cheese on top.

1,500 CALORIE MENU 4
no Fibre-Filler

	Calories	Fibre (g)
Daily allowances: two items of fruit, 1 pint (570ml) skimmed milk	300	5
Breakfast 2oz (55g) Kellogg's Sultana Bran with milk from allowance		
1 large thin slice wholemeal bread (1¼oz, 35g) spread with ¼oz (7g) low-fat spread and Marmite or yeast extract	275	10
Mid-morning snack An apple or pear from allowance		
Lunch 2 frozen beefburgers, grilled 4oz (115g) canned baked beans in tomato sauce		
An orange from allowance	330	8
After-school snack 1 large thin slice wholemeal bread (1¼oz, 35g) spread with ¼oz (7g) low-fat spread and 2 level teaspoons honey or jam	130	3
Evening meal * Individual Shepherd's Pie 4oz (115g) cabbage, boiled	425	9·5
Bed-time drink A cup of chocolate – 2 rounded teaspoons drinking chocolate with milk from allowance	40	0
TOTAL	1,500	35·5

* **Individual Shepherd's Pie**

Serves 1

4oz (115g) lean minced beef
1 small onion, finely chopped
2oz (55g) carrot, grated
1 level teaspoon plain flour
salt and freshly ground pepper
2½fl oz (70ml) beef stock made from ¼ beef stock cube
1 level tablespoon tomato purée
1oz (30g) cooked peas
6oz (170g) cooked potato, mashed
¼oz (7g) low-fat spread
1 tablespoon skimmed milk from allowance (optional)

Fry the minced beef in a pan until well browned, then drain off and discard fat which has cooked out of the meat. Add the onion, carrot, flour and salt and pepper to taste, to the meat in the pan. Blend the stock with the tomato purée and stir into the meat and vegetables. Heat to boiling point, stirring continuously, then cook for 5 minutes until the mixture thickens. Stir in the peas. Spoon into a small ovenproof dish. Cream the mashed potato with the low-fat spread and milk, if used. Spoon on top of the meat and fork the top. Bake at 200°C (400°F, gas 6), for 30 minutes or until the top is browned.

1,500 CALORIE MENU 5
no Fibre-Filler

	Calories	Fibre (g)
Daily allowances: two items of fruit, 1 pint (570ml) skimmed milk	300	5
Breakfast		
1oz (30g) Bran Flakes with ½oz (15g) chopped dried apricots (no-need-to-soak variety) and milk from allowance		
1 egg (size 3), poached and served on 1 large thin slice (1½oz, 35g) wholemeal bread, toasted, no butter	260	10

	Calories	Fibre (g)
Mid-morning snack		
An orange from allowance		
Lunch		
* Cottage Cheese and Piccalilli Sandwiches		
4oz (115g) carrot, cut into sticks		
150g carton fruit-flavoured yogurt	350	10·5
After-school snack		
An apple or pear from allowance		
Evening meal		
* Macaroni and Vegetable Cheese Bake		
Green salad: a few lettuce leaves, shredded,		
1oz (30g) sliced or diced cucumber, ½ small		
green pepper, chopped, and a few sprigs of		
watercress		
1 frozen chocolate éclair, thawed	550	12.5
Bed-time drink		
A cup of chocolate – 2 rounded teaspoons		
drinking chocolate with milk from		
allowance	40	0
TOTAL	1,500	38

* Cottage Cheese and Piccalilli Sandwiches

Serves 1

2oz (55g) cottage cheese (natural, with chives or with onion and
    peppers)
1oz (30g) piccalilli, chopped
2 large thin slices (1½oz, 35g each) wholemeal bread

Mix the cottage cheese with the piccalilli and sandwich between
the two slices of bread. Cut into four.

* Macaroni and Vegetable Cheese Bake

Serves 1

1½oz (45g) wholewheat macaroni
4oz (115g) frozen mixed vegetables
½oz (15g) wholemeal flour
¼ pint (140ml) skimmed milk from
    allowance
¼oz (7g) low-fat spread
salt and pepper
¼ teaspoon made mustard
1oz (30g) Cheddar cheese, grated

Boil the macaroni in lightly salted water for 12 minutes or until just tender. Drain well. Cook the vegetables as directed and drain. Put the flour, milk and low-fat spread in a saucepan and heat, whisking continuously until it boils and thickens. Season to taste with salt and pepper. Add the mustard and half the cheese. Stir the macaroni and vegetables into the sauce. Turn into an ovenproof dish. Sprinkle over the remaining cheese. Cook in a moderately hot oven (200°C, 400°F, gas 6) for 20 minutes or until the cheese is browned.

1,500 CALORIE MENU   6
no Fibre-Filler

	Calories	Fibre (g)
Daily allowances: two items of fruit, 1 pint (570ml) skimmed milk	300	5
Breakfast 1oz (30g) Bran Flakes with milk from allowance		
1 average-sized banana (6oz, 170g)	165	7·5

	Calories	Fibre (g)
Mid-morning snack		
1 Quaker Harvest Crunch Bar. almond or peanut		
An apple or pear from allowance	90	1
Lunch		
8oz (225g) canned baked beans in tomato sauce on 1 large thin slice (1¼oz, 35g) wholemeal bread, toasted	235	19·5
After-school snack		
150g carton fruit-flavoured yogurt	120	0
Evening meal		
* Oven-Baked Chicken and Chips		
2 average-sized tomatoes		
A bunch of watercress		
An orange from allowance	530	5·5
Bed-time snack and drink		
1 Hovis digestive biscuit		
Orange Milky – 1fl oz (30ml) low-calorie orange squash with ¼ pint (140ml) skimmed milk from allowance	60	0·5
TOTAL	1,500	39

* Oven-Baked Chicken and Chips

Serves 1

8oz (225g) chicken joint
salt and pepper
6oz (170g) frozen oven chips

Season the chicken joint well, and wrap in foil to form a parcel.

Bake in a hot oven (220°C, 425°F, gas 7), for 45 minutes or until tender. Place the chips on a baking tray and bake with the chicken for the last 15–20 minutes. Unwrap the chicken and remove and discard the skin. Serve with the chips.

1,500 CALORIE MENU 7
no Fibre-Filler

	Calories	Fibre (g)
Daily allowances: two items of fruit, 1 pint (570ml) skimmed milk	300	5
Breakfast 2oz (55g) Kellogg's Sultana Bran with milk from allowance	165	7
Mid-morning snack 1oz (30g) peanuts, mixed with 1oz (30g) raisins	230	4·5
Lunch * 2 Peanut Butter and Cress Snack Rolls 2oz (55g) carrot, cut into sticks An apple or pear from allowance	365	11
After-school snack 1 Quaker Harvest Crunch Bar, almond or peanut	90	1
Evening meal 6oz (170g) cod or haddock fillets brushed with ½oz (7g) low-fat spread and grilled 1 tomato, halved, grilled without fat 5oz (140g) boiled potato, mashed with 2 tablespoons milk from allowance 3oz (85g) frozen peas, cooked	310	9

	Calories	Fibre (g)
Bed-time drink:		
A cup of chocolate – 2 rounded teaspoons drinking chocolate with skimmed milk from allowance	40	0
TOTAL	1,500	37·5

*Peanut Butter and Cress Snack Rolls

Serves 1

2 wholemeal snack rolls (1½oz, 45g each)
1oz (30g) peanut butter
1 carton mustard and cress

Split the two rolls lengthwise. Spread one half of each roll with peanut butter and top with mustard and cress. Replace the remaining half of each roll.

1,500 CALORIE MENU   8
no Fibre-Filler

	Calories	Fibre (g)
Daily allowances: two items of fruit, 1 pint (570ml) skimmed milk	300	5
Breakfast		
1½oz (45g) Allinson Crunchy Bran with ½oz (15g) sultanas and milk from allowance		
1 Ryvita crispbread spread with ¼oz (7g) low-fat spread and 1 level teaspoon honey or marmalade	200	13·5

	Calories	Fibre (g)
Mid-morning snack 2 Hovis digestive biscuits		
An orange from allowance	110	1·5
Lunch 1 egg (size 3), poached and served on 1 large thin slice (1¼oz, 35g) wholemeal bread, toasted and spread with ¼oz (7g) low-fat spread		
* Apricot Yogurt Dessert	380	12
After-school snack 1 frozen choc bar (ice-cream) *or* 3oz (85g) vanilla ice-cream	150	0
Evening meal * Liver and Mushroom Filled Jacket Potato 4oz (115g) canned tomatoes 4oz (115g) cabbage, boiled	360	9·5
Bed-time snack An apple or pear from allowance		
TOTAL	1,500	41·5

* Apricot Yogurt Dessert

Serves 1

150g carton low-fat natural yogurt
2oz (55g) dried apricots (no-need-to-soak variety), chopped
1 teaspoon clear honey

Mix the yogurt, chopped apricots and honey together. Leave to stand for at least 30 minutes to allow flavours to blend.

* **Liver and Mushroom Filled Jacket Potato**

Serves 1

7oz (200g) potato
4oz (115g) chicken livers, chopped
1 tablespoon finely chopped onion
1oz (30g) mushrooms, sliced
5 tablespoons skimmed milk from allowance
salt and pepper
a dash of Worcestershire sauce

Scrub the potato well and bake (see p. 31). Meanwhile place the chicken livers, onion, mushrooms and milk in a small pan. Heat to simmering point, cover and cook gently for 5 minutes. Cut the potato in half lengthwise and scoop out some of the flesh. Mix the flesh with the chicken liver mixture. Season to taste and add the Worcestershire sauce. Pile back into the potato jackets. Heat through in the oven for 5–10 minutes, if necessary.

1,500 CALORIE MENU 9
no Fibre-Filler

	Calories	Fibre (g)
Daily allowances: two items of fruit, 1 pint (570ml) skimmed milk	300	5
Breakfast 1½oz (45g) Allinson Crunchy Bran, topped with average-sized (6oz, 170g) banana, sliced, with milk from allowance	210	16
Mid-morning snack 1 small packet (25g) crisps, any flavour	130	3
Lunch * Tuna and Celery Sandwiches An apple or pear from allowance	215	7

	Calories	Fibre (g)
After-school snack		
2 Boots Second Nature Biscuits, any variety		
An orange from allowance	80	1
Evening meal		
* Chicken Risotto		
2 Ryvita crispbreads with ½oz (7g) low-fat spread and 1oz (30g) Edam cheese	490	7·5
Bed-time drink		
Milk shake – 1 sachet Kellogg's Two Shakes, any flavour, with milk from allowance	75	0
TOTAL	1,500	39·5

* Tuna and Celery Sandwiches

Serves 1

1oz (30g) canned tuna in brine, drained
1 stick celery, finely chopped
1 tablespoon low-calorie salad dressing
a pinch of curry powder (optional)
2 large thin slices (1½oz. 35g each) wholemeal bread

Mash the tuna with a fork. then mix with the celery, salad dressing and curry powder, if used. Spread the tuna mixture on one slice of bread and top with the second slice. Cut diagonally into two or four.

* Chicken Risotto

Serves 1

2oz (55g) brown rice
1oz (30g) onion, finely chopped
2oz (55g) mushrooms, sliced

½ small green pepper, deseeded and chopped
1 tomato, skinned and chopped
½ chicken stock cube
a pinch of mixed herbs
salt and pepper
2oz (55g) cooked chicken

Place the rice, onion, mushrooms, pepper and tomato in a pan. Dissolve the stock cube in 8fl oz (225ml) boiling water and pour into the pan. Bring to the boil, add the mixed herbs and salt and pepper to taste. Stir well, reduce heat, cover and simmer until the stock is absorbed and the rice is tender, about 25 minutes. Remove any skin from the chicken and dice. Stir the chicken into the rice mixture and heat through gently for 5 minutes. Serve hot.

1,500 CALORIE MENU 10
no Fibre-Filler

	Calories	Fibre (g)
Daily allowances: two items of fruit, 1 pint (570ml) skimmed milk	300	5
Breakfast 2oz (55g) Kellogg's Sultana Bran with milk from allowance	165	7
Mid-morning snack 2 Boots Second Nature Biscuits, any variety	80	1
Lunch 2 frozen fish fingers, grilled without fat 8oz (225g) canned baked beans in tomato sauce An apple or pear from allowance	270	16·5
After-school snack 2oz (55g) slice fruit cake	200	1·5

	Calories	Fibre (g)
Evening meal		
* Cheese and Potato Pie		
* Raisin and Honey Stuffed Baked Apple	445	13
Bed-time drink		
A cup of chocolate – 2 rounded teaspoons drinking chocolate with milk from allowance	40	0
TOTAL	1,500	44

* Cheese and Potato Pie

Serves 1

6oz (170g) potato, peeled (weighed after peeling)
1 small onion (2oz, 55g), peeled and thinly sliced
1oz (30g) Cheddar cheese, grated
1oz (30g) sweetcorn kernels
salt and pepper
¼ pint (140ml) skimmed milk from allowance
½ level teaspoon Marmite or yeast extract

Slice the potato thinly. Arrange half the potato slices in the bottom of a small ovenproof dish. Top with half the sliced onion and half the cheese. Sprinkle over the sweetcorn. Season with salt and pepper to taste. Repeat the layers, using up the remaining potato, onion and cheese. Heat the milk and stir in the yeast extract. Pour over the cheese and vegetables. Cover and cook at 160°C (325°F, gas 3), for 1 hour. Serve hot.

* Raisin and Honey Stuffed Baked Apple

Serves 1

8oz (225g) cooking apple
1oz (30g) stoned raisins
1 teaspoon clear honey

Wash the apple and remove the core, leaving a hole for the filling.

Cut through the skin round the centre of the apple with a sharp knife to prevent it bursting during cooking. Place the apple in a small ovenproof dish. Mix the raisins with the honey and fill the hole with the raisins. Pour 2–4 tablespoons water round the apple. Cover with a lid or foil and bake at 160°C (325°F, gas 3) with the Cheese and Potato Pie for 45 minutes or until the apple is tender right through, but not overcooked. Serve hot or cold.

F-PLAN MENUS FOR FREEZER-OWNER COOKS

The inventor of the home freezer inadvertently invented the best slimming aid ever. Here's how to use it to maximum advantage, whether you cook and store F-Plan meals (pp. 247–64) or prefer to buy and store ready frozen convenience foods and follow the menus in the chapter on 'Canned and Packaged F-Plan Menus' (p. 156).

An enormously helpful way of ensuring that you stick to your diet is to plan ahead and prepare and store most of the foods you will need. One of the many advantages of this strategy is that when you start dieting you will be able to spend much less time in the kitchen, where the biscuit tin, bread bin and fridge door all seem to beckon to you, weakening your resolve. You are off to a head start if you stock your freezer with most if not all the sauces, soups, pizzas, flans, meat dishes and puds, packed in individual portions; you will then avoid all temptation to eat the wrong thing because you did not have time to shop for and cook the right thing.

The recipes for all the freezable dishes are given before the menus and not scattered throughout as in other sections, because freezer owners usually 'batch' cook in advance and then store the food until the day on which it is to be eaten. Recipes for four savoury sauces have been included, which can be used to liven up fish, meat and eggs with minimal effort. In addition to the home-cooked frozen foods in the menus one or two other foods commonly found in freezers – for example, ice-cream and frozen fruit, vegetables and fish – have been included. Should you be concerned that all the foods in these menus come from the freezer and that nothing is fresh, it will be reassuring to know that the menus follow all the basic F-Plan diet rules (p. 23) and contain the daily allowances of one portion of Fibre-Filler, an orange and an apple or pear and $\frac{1}{2}$ pint (285ml) skimmed milk. The menus also contain fresh bread, other fresh fruits, fresh vegetables, eggs, cheese and some fresh meat.

The menus are divided up into two parts; 1,000 calories and 1,250 calories daily, all providing 35–50g fibre.

Instructions have been included for reheating the frozen dishes in a microwave oven, as this is a particularly quick and convenient way of cooking or reheating frozen food.

SPECIAL DIET NOTES

1. Begin by deciding which daily calorie total will give you a satisfactory weight loss (p. 26).

2. Select the menus from your chosen daily calorie total for at least one week, preferably two or more, so that you can plan which dishes you need to prepare in advance and freeze. Remember to vary the menus and hence the foods to ensure that you are eating all the nutrients you need for good health.

3. Carry out as much cooking in advance of starting the diet as you can and have the dishes ready frozen in single portions.

4. Begin each day with Fibre-Filler (recipe on p. 24) from the daily allowance which you can prepare in 'batch' quantities too, if you wish.

5. Drink as much tea and coffee without sugar (artificial sweeteners can be used) as you wish each day, but remember to use only the skimmed milk from the daily allowance. In addition, drink as much water and drinks labelled 'low-calorie' as you wish. Alcoholic drinks have not been included in these menus. However, should you find it impossible to follow a diet which does not allow an occasional alcoholic drink, and if you are achieving a good weight loss, then you could try allowing yourself an increased calorie intake by selecting drinks from the chart (p. 285). However, it would be advisable to limit these to a daily total of 200 calories and if your weight loss stops then it will be necessary to leave out the drinks.

SAUCES

TOMATO SAUCE (30 calories, 2·5g fibre per portion)

6 portions

two 14oz (400g) cans tomatoes
1 large onion (6oz, 170g), peeled and chopped
1 large carrot (4oz, 115g), peeled and grated

1 stick celery
1 bay leaf
salt and pepper

Place all the ingredients in a medium-sized saucepan with $\frac{1}{4}$ pint (140ml) water, bring to the boil, reduce the heat and simmer for 20 minutes. Remove the bay leaf and purée the sauce, either through a sieve or in a blender. Season to taste.

To freeze
Leave to cool; divide equally between six polythene bags or individual freezer containers, seal, label and freeze.

To serve
Leave at room temperature for at least 3 hours, turn out into a saucepan and heat gently until piping hot.
  or
Turn out frozen portion on to a dish, cover with cling film and microwave on HIGH for 1½ minutes; remove from the oven and break up using a fork. Microwave on HIGH for a further 1½ minutes.

BARBECUE SAUCE (40 calories, 1g fibre per portion)

6 portions

8oz (225g) unsweetened apple purée
6 level tablespoons tomato purée
2 teaspoons vinegar
2 teaspoons Worcestershire sauce
4 level teaspoons sugar
4oz (115g) mushrooms, finely chopped
salt and pepper
Place all the ingredients in a medium-sized saucepan, with 1 pint (570ml) water, bring to the boil, reduce the heat and simmer for 20 minutes. Season to taste.

To freeze
Leave to cool; divide equally between six polythene bags or individual freezer containers, seal, label and freeze.

To serve

Leave at room temperature for at least 2½ hours, turn out into a saucepan and heat gently until piping hot.

or

Turn out frozen portion on to a dish, cover with cling film and microwave on HIGH for 1½ minutes; remove from the oven and break up using a fork. Microwave on HIGH for a further 1½ minutes.

SWEET AND SOUR SAUCE (85 calories, 1g fibre per portion)

4 portions

8oz (225g) canned pineapple pieces in natural juice
1 tablespoon clear honey
1 tablespoon vinegar
2 level tablespoons cornflour
3 tablespoons soy sauce
1 green pepper (4oz, 115g after removing seeds), cut into thin strips
2oz (55g) carrot, peeled and cut into thin strips
salt and pepper

Drain the pineapple, reserving the juice. Make the juice up to 1 pint (570ml) with water, place in a saucepan with the honey and vinegar. Mix the cornflour and soy sauce together, add to the water and bring to the boil, stirring continuously. When it thickens, add the vegetables and pineapple, reduce the heat and simmer for 20–25 minutes.

To freeze

Leave to cool; divide equally between four polythene bags or individual freezer containers, seal, label and freeze.

To serve

Leave at room temperature for at least 3 hours, turn out into a saucepan and heat gently until piping hot.

or

Turn out frozen portion on to a dish, cover with cling film and microwave on HIGH for 1½ minutes; remove from the oven and break up using a fork. Microwave on HIGH for a further 1½ minutes.

CURRY SAUCE (100 calories, 3·5g fibre per portion)

6 portions

1 large onion (6oz, 170g), peeled and chopped
1 large stick celery, finely chopped
1 teaspoon vegetable oil
1 level tablespoon curry powder
2 level tablespoons piccalilli
1 cooking apple (8oz, 225g), peeled, cored and chopped
3oz (85g) dried lentils
1oz (30g) sultanas
1 tablespoon lemon juice

Gently fry the onion and celery in the oil for 3–4 minutes. Add the curry powder and piccalilli, mix well. Add ¾ pint (425ml) water and bring to the boil. Add the apple, lentils, sultanas and lemon juice, bring back to the boil, reduce the heat and simmer for 25–30 minutes or until the lentils are soft.

To freeze
Leave to cool; divide between six ¼ pint (140ml) containers (for example, empty yogurt cartons). Cover and seal, label and freeze.

To serve
Thaw at room temperature for at least 3 hours empty into a saucepan and heat gently until piping hot.
    or
Turn out frozen portion on to a dish, cover with cling film and microwave on HIGH for 1½ minutes. Remove and break up using a fork. Microwave on HIGH for a further 1½ minutes.

SOUPS

CREAMY PEA SOUP (90 calories, 7·5g fibre per portion)

5 portions

1lb (455g) fresh or frozen peas
1 large onion (6oz, 170g), peeled and chopped
1 tablespoon chopped fresh mint *or* 1 level teaspoon dried mint
1¾ pints (1l) chicken stock made from 2 chicken stock cubes
1 level teaspoon sugar
salt and pepper
1oz (30g) low-fat skimmed milk powder

Place the peas, onion, mint, stock and sugar in a saucepan. Season with salt and pepper. Bring to the boil, cover and simmer for 30 minutes. Purée in a blender or rub through a sieve. Blend the skimmed milk powder with a little of the soup and return to the saucepan with the remaining soup. Reheat gently without boiling.

To freeze
Leave to cool; divide equally between five ½ pint (285ml) containers. Cover, label and freeze.

To serve
Thaw at room temperature for 2 hours, turn into a saucepan and heat gently until piping hot.
   or
Turn out frozen portion into a bowl, cover with cling film and microwave on HIGH for 2 minutes; remove and break up using a fork. Microwave on HIGH for a further 2 minutes until piping hot.

CARROT AND LENTIL SOUP (120 calories, 7·5g fibre per portion)

4 portions

1¼ pints (565ml) chicken stock, made with 1 stock cube
12oz (340g) carrots, peeled and sliced
4oz (115g) lentils

1 large onion (6oz, 170g), peeled and chopped
1 stick celery
2 teaspoons lemon juice
1 tablespoon chopped parsley
salt and pepper

In a large saucepan bring the chicken stock to the boil. Add the carrots, lentils, onion and celery, and simmer for 25 minutes or until the vegetables are tender. Remove from the heat and purée through a sieve or in a blender. Return to the saucepan and add the lemon juice and parsley; season with salt and pepper to taste.

To freeze
Leave to cool; divide equally between four ½ pint (285ml) containers, cover, label and freeze.

To serve
Thaw at room temperature for at least 2½ hours. Empty soup into a saucepan and heat gently until piping hot.
  or
Turn out frozen portion into a bowl, cover with cling film and microwave on HIGH for 5 minutes, stirring after 2 and 4 minutes.

SWEETCORN POTAGE (155 calories, 5·5g fibre per portion)

6 portions

1½ pints (850ml) chicken stock, made with 2 chicken stock
  cubes
1lb 4oz (565g) potatoes, peeled and diced
1 large onion (6oz, 170g), peeled and chopped
10oz (285g) canned sweetcorn
4oz (115g) mushrooms, sliced
1 green pepper, deseeded and chopped
1oz (30g) low-fat dried milk powder
salt and pepper

Put the stock in a large saucepan and bring to the boil. Add the potatoes, onion, sweetcorn, mushrooms and green pepper, and simmer for 30 minutes or until the vegetables are soft. Remove from the heat and allow to cool slightly; gradually stir in the milk powder. Season. Return to the heat and gently bring back to boiling point.

To freeze
Leave to cool; divide equally between six ½ pint (285ml) containers, cover, label and freeze.

To serve
Thaw at room temperature for at least 2½ hours, empty into a saucepan and heat gently until piping hot.
or
Turn out frozen portion into a bowl, cover with cling film and microwave on HIGH for 5 minutes, stirring after 2 and 4 minutes.

MAIN DISHES

COURGETTE AND SWEETCORN FLAN (225 calories, 4g fibre per portion)

6 portions

Pastry
6oz (170g) wholemeal flour
3oz (85g) low-fat spread

Filling
3oz (85g) onion, peeled and thinly sliced
3oz (85g) canned sweetcorn kernels
6oz (170g) courgette, thinly sliced
1 egg (size 2)
¼ pint (140ml) skimmed milk
¼ teaspoon mustard powder
salt and pepper
2oz (55g) mature Cheddar cheese, grated

Put the flour into a bowl and rub in the low-fat spread until the mixture resembles breadcrumbs. Stir in 3 tablespoons water and gather the dough together into a ball. Roll out the pastry (between two sheets of greaseproof paper for easier handling, if wished) and line an 8 inch (20cm) flan tin. Line the flan pastry with greaseproof paper and add some baking beans or bread crusts. Bake at 220°C (425°F, gas 7), for 10 minutes. Lift out the paper and beans and return the flan pastry to the oven for a further 5 minutes. Turn the oven down to 180°C (350°F, gas 4). Arrange the onion and sweetcorn in the bottom of the flan case. Arrange the courgette slices in overlapping circles on top of the sweetcorn and onion. Beat the egg, milk, mustard powder and salt and pepper together. Pour into the flan case. Bake in the oven for 15 minutes, then remove. Sprinkle the grated cheese over the top and return to the oven for a further 20 minutes or until the egg mixture is set and the cheese browned.

To freeze
Cool quickly, then cut into six equal pieces. Wrap each piece in foil, label and freeze.

To serve
Loosen foil wrapping and thaw at room temperature for 3 hours.

MEAT AND VEGETABLE LOAF (220 calories, 6g fibre per portion)

6 portions

4oz (115g) lentils
12oz (340g) lean minced beef
1 large onion, (6oz, 170g), peeled and chopped
4oz (115g) carrot, grated
6oz (170g) wholemeal breadcrumbs
3 level tablespoons tomato purée
1 level teaspoon mixed dried herbs
salt and pepper

Bring the lentils to the boil in ½ pint (285ml) water, then simmer gently for 25 minutes or until the lentils are soft. Preheat the oven to 180°C (350°F, gas 4). Lightly grease the sides of a 2lb (1 kg) loaf tin and place a piece of greaseproof or Bakewell paper in the bottom. Mix all the ingredients in a large bowl until they are evenly distributed. Put the mixture into the loaf tin; press down firmly using the back of a spoon. Bake in the middle of the oven for 1½ hours or until the meat loaf is brown and firm to the touch.

To freeze
Leave to cool in the tin; turn out and cut into twelve slices. Pack two slices (separated by a piece of greaseproof paper) into six polythene bags or individual freezer containers; seal, label and freeze.

To serve
Thaw at room temperature for at least 3½ hours; then either heat through in a hot oven or heat under the grill.
or
Turn out the frozen slices on to a dish, cover with cling film and microwave on HIGH for 2 minutes, turn over and microwave for a further 2 minutes.

SARDINE AND TOMATO PIZZA (265 calories, 5g fibre per portion)

5 portions

8oz (225g) wholemeal flour
1 level teaspoon salt
½oz (15g) low-fat spread
1 sachet Harvest Gold Easy Blend Yeast

Topping
1 level tablespoon tomato purée
4½oz (130g) canned sardines in tomato sauce
1 large onion (6oz, 170g), peeled and thinly sliced
6oz (170g) tomatoes, sliced
3oz (85g) Edam cheese, grated
½ teaspoon dried basil

Put the flour, salt and low-fat spread into a large mixing bowl and rub together until the mixture resembles breadcrumbs. Stir in the yeast and add ¼ pint (140ml) warm water to form a soft dough. Knead the dough for 5–7 minutes until smooth. Leave to prove (rise) in a lightly oiled polythene bag for 30 minutes or until it has doubled in size. Divide the dough into 5 portions, roll out each one to fit a 6 inch (15cm) round freezer container. Spread the tomato purée over them. Mash the sardines together with their sauce and place evenly over the tomato purée. Place the onion, tomato and cheese on each pizza, and sprinkle a little basil over the top.

To freeze
Open freeze, then when frozen, place with the container in a polythene bag, seal, label and freeze.

To serve
Defrost at room temperature for at least 2 hours, place in a pre-heated oven, 200°C (400°F, gas 6), for 15 minutes or until base is crusty.

BEEF AND BEAN CASSEROLE (195 calories, 6g fibre per portion)

4 portions

12oz (340g) stewing steak, fat removed, cut into 1 inch
   (2.5cm) cubes
1 large onion (6oz, 170g), peeled and chopped
1 large carrot (3oz, 85g), peeled and sliced
8oz (225g) canned baked beans in tomato sauce
1oz (30g) pearl barley
½ pint (285ml) beef stock, using 1 beef stock cube
1 teaspoon Worcestershire sauce
1 teaspoon vinegar
salt and pepper

Preheat the oven to 160°C (325°F, gas 3). Place the meat in a 2 pint (1l) ovenproof dish with the onion, carrot, baked beans and pearl barley. Mix together the beef stock, Worcestershire sauce and vinegar and pour over the meat. Season with salt and pepper. Cover and bake in the middle of the oven for 2 hours or until the meat and carrot are tender.

To freeze

Leave to cool; then divide equally between four polythene bags or four individual freezer containers. Seal, label and freeze.

To serve

Thaw at room temperature for at least 4 hours, empty into a saucepan and heat gently until piping hot.

or

Turn out frozen portion on to a dish. Cover with cling film and microwave on HIGH for 2 minutes; remove from the microwave and break up using a fork. Microwave on HIGH for a further 1½ minutes.

CHILI CON CARNE (245 Calories, 9·5g fibre per portion)

4 portions

4oz (115g) red kidney beans, soaked overnight in water
1 large onion (6oz, 170g), peeled and chopped
8oz (225g) lean minced beef
2 large sticks celery, finely chopped
4oz (115g) mushrooms, sliced
2 level tablespoons tomato purée
1–2 level teaspoons chili powder, or to taste
14oz (400g) canned tomatoes
salt and pepper

Bring the kidney beans to the boil in lightly salted water and boil rapidly for 15 minutes; remove from the heat and drain. Gently fry the onion and minced beef, without added fat, for 2 to 3 minutes. To the meat mixture add the celery, mushrooms, tomato purée and chili powder, and mix thoroughly until the ingredients are evenly distributed. Pour in the tomatoes and ¼ pint (140ml) water, and add the kidney beans. Stir until the mixture is boiling. Reduce heat, cover and leave to simmer gently for approximately 1 hour or until the kidney beans are tender.

To freeze

Leave to cool; then divide equally between four polythene bags or four individual freezer containers. Seal, label and freeze.

To serve

Thaw at room temperature for at least 4 hours. Empty into a saucepan and heat gently until piping hot.

or

Turn out frozen portion on to a dish. Cover with cling film and microwave on HIGH for 1½ minutes; remove from the microwave and break up using a fork. Microwave on HIGH for a further 1½ minutes.

FILLET OF PORK WITH PRUNES (260 calories, 6g fibre per portion)

4 portions

1lb (455g) lean pork fillet, fat removed, cut into 1 inch
    (2·5cm) cubes
4oz (115g) dried prunes, soaked overnight and
    drained
2oz (55g) raisins
1 cooking apple (8oz, 225g), cored and chopped
2 level tablespoons piccalilli

Preheat the oven to 180°C (350°F, gas 4). Place the meat in a 2 pint (1l) ovenproof dish with the prunes, raisins and apple. Mix the piccalilli with ½ pint (285ml) water and pour over the meat. Cover and bake in the middle of the oven for 1 hour or until the meat is tender.

To freeze

Leave to cool; then divide equally between four polythene bags or four individual freezer containers. Seal, label and freeze.

To serve

Thaw at room temperature for at least 4 hours, empty into a saucepan and heat gently until piping hot.

or

Turn out frozen portion on to a dish, cover with cling film and microwave on HIGH for 1½ minutes. Remove from the microwave and break up using a fork. Microwave on HIGH for a further 1½ minutes.

PAPRIKA CHICKEN (275 calories, 6g fibre per portion)

4 portions

2oz (55g) haricot beans, soaked overnight and drained
4 chicken pieces (weighing approximately 8oz, 225g each),
 skin removed
4oz (115g) frozen sweetcorn kernels
1oz (30g) brown rice
14oz (400g) canned tomatoes
¼ pint (140ml) chicken stock, made from ½ chicken stock
 cube
1 tablespoon vinegar
¼ teaspoon paprika

Preheat the oven to 190°C (375°F, gas 5). Place the haricot beans and skinned chicken pieces into a 3 pint (1¾ l) ovenproof dish with the sweetcorn, rice and canned tomatoes. Mix together the stock, vinegar and paprika, and pour over the chicken joints. Cover and bake in the middle of the oven for 50–55 minutes or until the chicken and rice are tender.

To freeze
Leave to cool, then divide equally between four polythene bags or four individual freezer containers. Seal, label and freeze.

To serve
Thaw at room temperature for at least 4 hours, empty into an ovenproof dish and reheat at 200°C (400°F, gas 6), for 35–40 minutes.
 or
Turn out frozen portion on to a dish, cover with cling film and microwave on HIGH for 2 minutes. Take the chicken out and turn it over. Cook for a further 2 minutes on HIGH. Repeat this twice more.

LAMB WITH SPLIT PEAS (290 calories, 5·5g fibre per portion)

4 portions

8oz (225g) lean shoulder of lamb (weighed without the bone),
    cut into 1 inch (2.5cm) cubes
4oz (115g) dried split peas, soaked overnight in water
1 large onion (6oz, 170g), peeled and chopped
8oz (225g) carrots, peeled and sliced
2 bay leaves
½ teaspoon ground nutmeg
¾ pint (425ml) beef stock, made from 1 beef stock cube

Preheat the oven to 160°C (325°F, gas 3). Gently fry the lamb in a
non-stick pan, without added fat, until lightly browned. Drain off
and discard any fat which has cooked out of the meat. Place meat
in a 2 pint (1l) ovenproof dish, with the rest of the ingredients.
Cover the dish and bake in the middle of the oven for 2–2¼ hours
until the meat and carrots are tender.

To freeze
Leave to cool; then divide equally between four polythene bags or
four individual freezer containers. Seal, label and freeze.

To serve
Thaw at room temperature for at least 4 hours, empty into a
saucepan and heat gently until piping hot.
    or
Turn out frozen portion on to a dish, cover with cling film and
microwave on HIGH for 1½ minutes. Remove and break up using
a fork. Microwave on HIGH for a further 1½ minutes.

PUDDINGS

PEAR AND APRICOT MOUSSE (110 calories, 2g fibre per
portion)

6 portions

14½oz (410g) can pears in natural or fruit juice
14½oz (410g) can apricots in natural or fruit juice

3 eggs (size 3), separated
1 teaspoon clear honey
1 envelope or 3 level teaspoons powdered gelatine

Reserve 3 tablespoons juice from the can of pears and purée the pears and apricots with the remaining juice. Beat the egg yolks and honey with 1 teaspoon hot water until pale and creamy. Place the gelatine in a small heatproof bowl with the reserved juice. Stand the bowl in a saucepan of water and heat until the gelatine is dissolved. Cool slightly; stir into the egg yolk mixture with the fruit purée. Whisk the egg whites until stiff and gently fold into the mixture.

To freeze
Pour the mousse into six ½ pint (285ml) containers (for example, cottage cheese cartons). Cover, label and freeze.

To serve
Place in the refrigerator for 2½–3 hours.

PLUM CHARLOTTE (135 calories, 5·5g fibre per portion)

6 portions

1lb (455g) dessert plums, stoned
4oz (115g) wholemeal breadcrumbs
2oz (55g) Quaker Harvest Crunch with Bran and Apple
¼ teaspoon ground cinnamon
grated rind of 1 orange
6 tablespoons fresh orange juice
2 level tablespoons soft brown sugar

Divide half the plums equally between six individual soufflé dishes or small foil basins and spread out over the bases. Mix the breadcrumbs, Harvest Crunch, cinnamon and grated orange rind together. Sprinkle half this mixture over the plums. Cover with the remaining plums, dividing them equally between the dishes and top with the remaining breadcrumb mixture. Mix the orange juice with the sugar and spoon an equal amount over the top of each charlotte. Stand the dishes on a baking tray and bake at 180°C (350°F, gas 4), for 30 minutes, until the top is crisp and browned. Serve hot.

To freeze
Cool as quickly as possible, cover with foil, label and freeze.

To serve
Thaw at room temperature for 2–3 hours, then heat through in the oven at 200°C (400°F, gas 6), for about 15 minutes or until hot.

RHUBARB AND BREAD PUDDING (150 calories, 4·5g fibre per portion)

6 portions

1lb 4oz (565g) rhubarb, cut into 1 inch (2.5cm) pieces
4 large slices (1¼oz, 35g each) wholemeal bread, each cut into
   9 squares
1oz (30g) sultanas
1½oz (35g) soft brown sugar
½ teaspoon ground ginger
¾ pint (425ml) skimmed milk
2 eggs (size 2)

Preheat the oven to 180°C (350°F, gas 4). Divide half the rhubarb between six individual freezer containers and cover each with three squares of bread. Sprinkle the sultanas over the bread and repeat the rhubarb and bread layers once more. Beat together the sugar, ginger, milk and eggs, and pour over the rhubarb and bread and leave to stand for 20–30 minutes. Bake in the oven for 30 minutes until the custard is set and rhubarb is soft.

To freeze
Leave to cool, cover, label and freeze.

To serve
Thaw at room temperature for 2 hours, uncover and then reheat at 200°C (400°F, gas 6) for about 15–20 minutes or until heated through.

TUTTI FRUTTI ICE-CREAM (155 calories, 3·5g fibre per portion)

1oz (30g) flaked almonds
1oz (30g) wholemeal breadcrumbs
¼ pint (285ml) natural low fat yogurt
2oz (55g) dried apricots, finely chopped
1oz (30g) raisins
3 egg whites (size 3)
3oz (85g) soft brown sugar

Toast the flaked almonds and breadcrumbs under a hot grill until golden brown. Add to the yogurt with the dried apricots and raisins. Whisk the egg whites until stiff, add the sugar and whisk again until stiff. Fold the yogurt mixture into the whisked egg whites and pour into a rigid plastic container (for example an ice-cream carton). Freeze until just solid. Cut into six equal portions, wrap individually in cling film and place in a polythene bag; replace in the freezer.

To serve
Place in a refrigerator for 20–30 minutes before serving to allow the ice-cream to soften slightly.

BLACKBERRY AND APPLE CRUMBLE (195 calories, 7·5g fibre per portion)

5 portions

Crumble topping
4oz (115g) wholemeal flour
2oz (55g) low-fat spread
1oz (30g) soft brown sugar
1oz (30g) desiccated coconut

Filling
8oz (225g) blackberries
8oz (225g) cooking apples, peeled, cored and sliced
1 teaspoon clear honey

Put the flour and low-fat spread into a mixing bowl and rub together until the mixture resembles breadcrumbs. Stir in the sugar and coconut and leave to one side. Mix the blackberries, apple slices and honey together, and divide between five individual foil basins or dishes. Divide the crumble topping between each portion of fruit.

To freeze
Cover the uncooked crumbles, label and freeze.

To serve
Leave to defrost at room temperature for 2 hours; uncover and cook in a preheated oven 200°C (400°F, gas 6), for about 20 minutes or until crumble topping is browned.

1,000 CALORIE MENU 1

	Calories	Fibre (g)
Daily allowance: Fibre-Filler; ½ pint (285ml) skimmed milk, two items of fruit	400	20

Breakfast
Half portion of Fibre-Filler with milk from allowance

An orange from allowance

Lunch
1 portion Sweetcorn Potage (p. 252)
1 frozen Birds Eye Cod, Coley or Haddock Steak
(Thaw the fish steak with the Sweetcorn Potage then heat the two together in a saucepan until the fish is cooked and can be flaked into the potage. Serve hot.)

An apple or pear from allowance	200	7·5

	Calories	Fibre (g)
Evening meal		
1 portion Fillet of Pork with Prunes		
(p. 258)		
4oz (115g) frozen Brussels sprouts, boiled		
2oz (55g) carrots, boiled		
1 portion Pear and Apricot Mousse		
(p. 260)	400	13
Snack		
Half portion of Fibre-Filler with milk from		
allowance		

TOTAL	1,000	40·5

1,000 CALORIE MENU 2

	Calories	Fibre (g)
Daily allowance: Fibre-Filler, ½ pint		
(285ml) skimmed milk, two items of		
fruit	400	20
Breakfast		
Half portion of Fibre-Filler with milk from		
allowance		
An apple or pear from allowance		
Lunch		
1 egg (size 3), poached and served on		
1 large thin slice (1¼oz, 35g) wholemeal		
bread, toasted and spread with ¼oz (7g)		
low-fat spread		
1 portion Tutti Frutti Ice-cream (p. 263)	335	6·5

	Calories	Fibre (g)
Evening meal 1 portion Chili Con Carne (p. 257) 4oz (115g) cabbage, boiled		
An orange from allowance	265	12·5
Snack Half portion of Fibre-Filler with milk from allowance		
TOTAL	1,000	39

1,000 CALORIE MENU   3

	Calories	Fibre (g)
Daily allowance: Fibre-Filler, ½ pint (285ml) skimmed milk, two items of fruit	400	20
Breakfast Half portion of Fibre-Filler with milk from allowance		
An orange from allowance		
Lunch 1 portion Carrot and Lentil Soup (p. 251) 2 Energen F-Plan Diet Brancrisps, with 1oz (30g) Edam cheese		
An apple or pear from allowance	255	10
Evening meal 1 bacon steak (3½oz, 100g raw weight), grilled without added fat 1 portion Sweet and Sour Sauce (p. 249) 3oz (85g) canned sweetcorn kernels 4oz (115g) cauliflower, boiled		
4oz (115g) fresh or frozen raspberries with 1oz (30g) vanilla ice-cream	345	16·5

	Calories	Fibre (g)

Snack
Half portion of Fibre-Filler with milk from
allowance

TOTAL	1,000	46·5

1,000 CALORIE MENU 4

	Calories	Fibre (g)
Daily allowance: Fibre-Filler, ½ pint (285ml) skimmed milk, two items of fruit	400	20

Breakfast
Half portion of Fibre-Filler with milk from
allowance

An apple or pear from allowance

Lunch
1 (2oz, 55g) frozen beefburger, well grilled,
served in a 2oz (55g) wholemeal lunch roll
with 1 tablespoon piccalilli
Small bunch watercress and 1
average-sized tomato

An orange from allowance	260	7

Evening meal
1 packet Birds Eye Smoked Cod in Butter
Sauce
6oz (170g) frozen mixed peas, sweetcorn
and peppers

4oz (115g) fresh or frozen blackcurrants or blackberries stewed with a little water and sweetened with ¼oz (7g) sugar	340	18·5/ 17·0

	Calories	Fibre (g)
Snack Half portion of Fibre-Filler with milk from allowance		
TOTAL	1,000	45·5/ 44·0

1,000 CALORIE MENU 5

	Calories	Fibre (g)
Daily allowance: Fibre-Filler, ½ pint (285ml) skimmed milk, two items of fruit	400	20

Breakfast
Half portion of Fibre-Filler with milk from allowance

An orange from allowance

Lunch
1 portion Creamy Pea Soup (p. 251)
1 rasher streaky bacon, well grilled and crumbled over the soup
1 Energen F-Plan Diet Brancrisp

An apple or pear from allowance	165	10

Evening meal
1 portion Lamb with Split Peas (p. 260)
4oz (115g) Brussels sprouts, boiled
4oz (115g) potatoes, boiled and mashed
with a little skimmed milk from
allowance

2oz (55g) green grapes	435	10·5

	Calories	Fibre (g)

Snack
Remaining portion of Fibre-Filler with milk
from allowance

	Calories	Fibre (g)
TOTAL	1,000	40·5

1,000 CALORIE MENU 6

	Calories	Fibre (g)
Daily allowance: Fibre-Filler, ½ pint (285ml) skimmed milk, two items of fruit	400	20

Breakfast
Half portion of Fibre-Filler with milk from
allowance

2oz (55g) green grapes	35	0·5

Lunch
1 portion Meat and Vegetable Loaf (p. 254)
heated with 1 portion of Tomato Sauce
(p. 247)
2oz (55g) white cabbage, shredded, mixed
with 2oz (55g) carrot, grated, and 1
tablespoon low-calorie salad dressing

An orange from allowance	300	11·5

Evening meal
1 portion Sweetcorn Potage (p. 252)
2oz (55g) frozen prawns, thawed
(Heat the Sweetcorn Potage with the
prawns until piping hot.)

1 Energen F-Plan Diet Brancrisp, spread
with 1oz (30g) cottage cheese (with chives
or with onion and peppers)

An apple or pear from allowance	265	7

	Calories	Fibre (g)
Snack Remaining portion of Fibre-Filler with milk from allowance		
TOTAL	1,000	39

1,000 CALORIE MENU 7

	Calories	Fibre (g)
Daily allowance: Fibre-Filler, ½ pint (285ml) skimmed milk, two items of fruit	400	20

Breakfast
Half portion of Fibre-Filler with milk from
allowance

Lunch
1 portion Courgette and Sweetcorn Flan
(p. 253)
2oz (55g) carrot sticks
2oz (55g) celery sticks

	Calories	Fibre (g)
An orange from allowance	240	6·5

Evening meal
1 portion Paprika Chicken (p. 259)
Half 10·6oz (300g) pack frozen cut-leaf
spinach, cooked without butter

1 Energen F-Plan Diet Brancrisp, spread
with 1oz (30g) cottage cheese (natural or
with chives or with onion and peppers or
with pineapple) and topped with 1oz (30g)
chopped green pepper or a few sprigs
watercress

	Calories	Fibre (g)
An apple or pear from allowance	360	17

	Calories	Fibre (g)

Snack
Remaining portion of Fibre-Filler with milk
from allowance

TOTAL	1,000	43·5

1,000 CALORIE MENU · 8

	Calories	Fibre (g)
Daily allowance: Fibre-Filler, ½ pint (285ml) skimmed milk, two items of fruit	400	20

Breakfast
Half portion of Fibre-Filler with milk from
allowance

Lunch
Curried egg on toast: 1 large thin slice
(1½oz, 35g) wholemeal bread, toasted
and topped with 1 egg (size 3), poached
and 1 portion of Curry Sauce (p. 250)
heated

An apple or pear from allowance	255	6·5

Evening meal
1 portion Meat and Vegetable Loaf
(p. 254), heated
4oz (115g) baked beans
4oz (115g) mushrooms, poached in
stock
or 7½oz (215g) canned button
mushrooms in brine

An orange from allowance	305	17

	Calories	Fibre (g)
Snack Remaining portion of Fibre-Filler with milk from allowance		
1 Boots Second Nature Wholemeal Muesli Fruit Biscuit	40	0·5
TOTAL	1,000	44

1,000 CALORIE MENU   9

	Calories	Fibre (g)
Daily allowance: Fibre-Filler, ½ pint (285ml) skimmed milk, two items of fruit	400	20
Breakfast Half portion of Fibre-Filler with milk from allowance		
An orange from allowance		
Lunch 1 portion Carrot and Lentil Soup (p. 251) 2 Energen F-Plan Diet Brancrisps, spread with Marmite or yeast extract		
An average-sized banana (6oz, 170g)	250	12·5
Evening meal 1 portion Beef and Bean Casserole (p. 256) 4oz (115g) cauliflower, boiled 2oz (55g) runner beans, boiled		
1 portion Plum Charlotte (p. 261)	350	15·5

	Calories	Fibre (g)
Snack Remaining portion of Fibre-Filler with milk from allowance		
An apple or pear from allowance		

TOTAL	1,000	48

1,000 CALORIE MENU   10

	Calories	Fibre (g)
Daily allowance: Fibre-Filler, ½ pint (285ml) skimmed milk, two items of fruit	400	20
Breakfast Half portion of Fibre-Filler with milk from allowance		
Lunch 1 Sardine and Tomato Pizza (p. 255) Green salad: a few lettuce leaves, a bunch of watercress, a few slices of cucumber, a few rings of green pepper and 1 tablespoon oil-free French dressing		
An orange from allowance	285	6·5
Evening meal 8oz (225g) chicken leg joint with all skin removed 1 portion Curry Sauce (p. 250), thawed (Cover the skinned chicken joint with the curry sauce and bake in a covered dish at 200°C, 400°F, gas 6, for 45 minutes or until the chicken is tender and cooked through.) 3oz (85g) frozen peas, boiled		
An apple or pear from allowance	315	10

	Calories	Fibre (g)
Snack Half portion of Fibre-Filler with milk from allowance		
TOTAL	1,000	36·5

1,250 CALORIE MENU 1

	Calories	Fibre (g)
Daily allowance: Fibre-Filler, ½ pint (285ml) skimmed milk, two items of fruit	400	20
Breakfast Half portion of Fibre-Filler with milk from allowance 1 large thin slice (1½oz, 35g) wholemeal bread, toasted and spread with ¼oz (7g) low-fat spread and 1 level teaspoon honey or marmalade	115	3
Lunch 1 Sardine and Tomato Pizza (p. 255) 2oz (55g) white cabbage, shredded, mixed with 2oz (55g) carrot, grated, and 1 tablespoon low-calorie salad dressing		
An apple or pear from allowance	315	8
Evening meal 1 portion Paprika Chicken (p. 259) 4oz (115g) potatoes, boiled and mashed with a little milk from allowance 4oz (115g) cabbage, boiled		
An orange from allowance	380	10·5

	Calories	Fibre (g)
Snack Remaining portion of Fibre-Filler with milk from allowance		
1 Boots Second Nature Wholemeal Muesli Fruit Biscuit	40	0·5

TOTAL	1,250	42

1,250 CALORIE MENU 2

	Calories	Fibre (g)
Daily allowance: Fibre-Filler, ½ pint (285ml) skimmed milk, two items of fruit	400	20
Breakfast Half portion of Fibre-Filler with milk from allowance 1 average-sized banana (6oz, 170g)	80	3·5
Lunch 1 portion Carrot and Lentil Soup (p. 251) 1 large thin slice (1¼oz, 35g) wholemeal bread, toasted and spread with Marmite or yeast extract, cut into fingers and served with the soup		
An apple or pear from allowance	200	10·5
Evening meal 7oz (200g) pork chop, grilled and fat trimmed off after grilling 1 portion Barbecue Sauce (p. 248), heated and served with pork chop 4oz (115g) frozen mixed peas, sweetcorn and peppers, boiled		

	Calories	Fibre (g)
1 portion Tutti Frutti Ice-cream (p. 263) served with an orange from allowance, segmented	570	11

Snack
Remaining portion of Fibre-Filler with milk from allowance

TOTAL	1,250	45

1,250 CALORIE MENU 3

	Calories	Fibre (g)
Daily allowance: Fibre-Filler, ½ pint (285ml) skimmed milk, two items of fruit	400	20

Breakfast
Half portion of Fibre-Filler with milk from allowance

2 Energen F-Plan Diet Brancrisps, spread with ¼oz (7g) low-fat spread and 2 level teaspoons honey or marmalade	100	4·5

Lunch
1 large thin slice (1¼oz, 35g) wholemeal bread, toasted and topped with 1 average-sized tomato, sliced, a pinch of mixed herbs and 1oz (30g) grated Edam cheese, then heated under grill until the cheese is melted

An apple or pear from allowance	170	4

Evening meal
1 portion Beef and Bean Casserole (p. 256)

	Calories	Fibre (g)
7oz (200g) potato baked in its jacket (see p. 31 for baking instructions) 4oz (115g) Brussels sprouts, boiled		
1 portion Blackberry and Apple Crumble (p. 263)	580	21·5

Snack
Remaining portion of Fibre-Filler with milk from allowance

An orange from allowance

TOTAL	1,250	50

1,250 CALORIE MENU 4

	Calories	Fibre (g)
Daily allowance: Fibre-Filler, ½ pint (285ml) skimmed milk, two items of fruit	400	20

Breakfast
Half portion of Fibre-Filler with milk from allowance

1 egg (size 3), boiled and served with 2 Energen F-Plan Diet Brancrisps, spread with ¼oz (7g) low-fat spread	150	2·5

Lunch
1 portion Sweetcorn Potage (p. 252)
1oz (30g) boiled lean ham, chopped
(Heat the Sweetcorn Potage and sprinkle over the chopped ham.)

1 large thin slice (1¼oz, 35g)

	Calories	Fibre (g)
wholemeal bread spread with 1 triangle cheese spread		
An orange from allowance	285	10·5

Evening meal
6oz (170g) cod or haddock fillet topped
with 1 portion Tomato Sauce (p. 247) and
baked in the oven at 180°C (350°F, gas 4),
for 20 minutes or until the fish is cooked
through
4oz (115g) frozen peas, boiled
4oz (115g) cauliflower, boiled

	Calories	Fibre (g)
1 portion Tutti Frutti Ice-cream (p. 263) served with an apple or pear from allowance, cored and sliced	375	16·5

Snack
Remaining portion of Fibre-Filler with milk
from allowance
1 Boots Second Nature Wholemeal Muesli

	Calories	Fibre (g)
Fruit Biscuit	40	0·5
TOTAL	1,250	50

1,250 CALORIE MENU   5

	Calories	Fibre (g)
Daily allowance: Fibre-Filler, ½ pint (285ml) skimmed milk, two items of fruit	400	20

Breakfast
Half portion of Fibre-Filler with milk from
allowance

An orange from allowance

	Calories	Fibre (g)

Lunch
2 frozen beefburgers, grilled and served
with 1 portion Barbecue Sauce (p. 248),
heated
4oz (115g) canned baked beans in tomato
sauce

An apple or pear from allowance	375	9

Evening meal
1 portion Fillet of Pork with Prunes (p. 258)
4oz (115g) cabbage, boiled

1 portion Rhubarb and Bread Pudding (p. 262) topped with 1oz (30g) vanilla ice-cream	475	13·5

Snack
Remaining portion of Fibre-Filler with milk
from allowance

TOTAL	1,250	42·5

1,250 CALORIE MENU   6

	Calories	Fibre (g)
Daily allowance: Fibre-Filler, ½ pint (285ml) skimmed milk, two items of fruit	400	20

Breakfast
Half portion of Fibre-Filler with milk from
allowance
1 large thin slice (1½oz, 35g) wholemeal
bread, toasted, spread with ¼oz (7g) low-fat
spread and 1 level teaspoon honey or

marmalade	115	3

	Calories	Fibre (g)

Lunch
1 portion Courgette and Sweetcorn Flan
(p. 253)
A bunch of watercress
2 average-sized tomatoes

An apple or pear from allowance

1 Boots Second Nature Wholemeal
Muesli Fruit Biscuit · 285 · 7

Evening meal
1 portion Chili con Carne (p. 257)
4oz (115g) cauliflower, boiled
2oz (55g) runner beans, boiled

1 portion Plum Charlotte (p. 257)
topped with 1oz (30g) vanilla ice-cream · 450 · 19

Snack
Remaining portion of Fibre-Filler with milk
from allowance

An orange from allowance

TOTAL	1,250	49

1,250 CALORIE MENU · 7

	Calories	Fibre(g)

Daily allowance. Fibre-Filler, ½ pint
(285ml) skimmed milk, two items of fruit · 400 · 20

Breakfast
Half portion of Fibre-Filler with milk from
allowance

1 average-sized banana (6oz, 170g) · 80 · 3·5

	Calories	Fibre (g)

Lunch
1 portion Creamy Pea Soup (p. 251)

Cottage cheese sandwich: 2 large thin
slices (1½oz, 35g each) wholemeal bread,
2 lettuce leaves, 2oz (55g) cottage cheese
(natural or with chives or with onion
and peppers or with pineapple)
(Arrange a lettuce leaf on 1 slice of bread,
top with the cottage cheese, the second
lettuce leaf and the second slice of bread.)

An orange from allowance	295	13·5

Evening meal
2 pork sausages (2oz, 55g each, raw
weight), grilled, served with 1 portion
Sweet and Sour Sauce (p. 249), heated
4oz (115g) cabbage, boiled
2oz (55g) canned sweetcorn kernels

An apple or pear from allowance	415	7·5

Snack
Remaining portion of Fibre-Filler with milk
from allowance

1 Energen F-Plan Diet Brancrisp, spread with 1 tablespoon low-calorie salad dressing, 1 tomato, sliced and a few slices cucumber	60	2

TOTAL	1,250	46·5

1,250 CALORIE MENU 8

	Calories	Fibre (g)
Daily allowance: Fibre-Filler, ½ pint (285ml) skimmed milk, two items of fruit	400	20

	Calories	Fibre (g)
Breakfast Half portion of Fibre-Filler with milk from allowance		
1 egg (size 3), boiled 2 Energen F-Plan Diet Brancrisps, spread with ¼oz (7g) low-fat spread	150	2·5
Lunch 1 Sardine and Tomato Pizza (p. 255) A small bunch of watercress 1oz (30g) pickled beetroot		
An apple or pear from allowance	280	6·5
Evening meal 1 portion Lamb with Split Peas (p. 260) 4oz (115g) Brussels sprouts, boiled		
1 portion Pear and Apricot Mousse (p. 260)	420	10·5
Snack Remaining portion of Fibre-Filler with milk from allowance		
An orange from allowance		
TOTAL	1,250	39·5

1,250 CALORIE MENU 9

	Calories	Fibre (g)
Daily allowance: Fibre-Filler, ½ pint (285ml) skimmed milk, two items of fruit	400	20
Breakfast Half portion of Fibre-Filler with milk from allowance		

	Calories	Fibre (g)
1 large thin slice (1½oz, 35g) wholemeal bread, toasted and spread with ½oz (7g) low-fat spread and Marmite or yeast extract	105	3

Lunch
1 portion Carrot and Lentil Soup (p. 251)
2 Energen F-Plan Diet Brancrisps, spread with 1 triangle cheese spread

An apple or pear from allowance	205	10

Evening meal
4oz (115g) lamb's liver, sliced and brushed with 1 teaspoon oil and grilled
1 portion Sweet and Sour Sauce (p. 249)
4oz (115g) Birds Eye Frozen Rice, Peas and Mushrooms, cooked without added butter

An orange from allowance	500	6

Snack
Remaining portion of Fibre-Filler with milk from allowance

1 Boots Second Nature Wholemeal Muesli Fruit Biscuit	40	0·5

TOTAL	1,250	39·5

1,250 CALORIE MENU 10

	Calories	Fibre (g)
Daily allowance: Fibre-Filler, ½ pint (285ml) skimmed milk, two items of fruit	400	20

	Calories	Fibre (g)

Breakfast
Half portion of Fibre-Filler with milk from
allowance

| 1 large banana (7oz, 200g) | 95 | 4 |

Lunch
Prawn sandwich: 2 large thin slices (1½oz,
35g each) wholemeal bread, spread with 1
tablespoon low-calorie salad dressing and
filled with 1oz (30g) frozen prawns,
thawed, 1 tomato, sliced, and a few sprigs
of watercress

| An apple or pear from allowance | 215 | 7 |

Evening meal
2 frozen Birds Eye Cod, Coley or Haddock
Steaks, thawed and covered with 1 portion
Curry Sauce (p. 250) and baked in the
oven in a covered dish at 190°C (375°F,
gas 5) for 25 minutes or until the fish is
cooked through
4oz (115g) mushrooms, poached in stock
or 7½oz (215g) canned button mushrooms
in brine
4oz (115g) runner beans, boiled

| 1 portion Blackberry and Apple Crumble
(p. 263) topped with 1oz (30g) vanilla
ice-cream | 540 | 18 |

Snack
Remaining portion of Fibre-Filler with milk
from allowance

An orange from allowance

| TOTAL | 1,250 | 49 |

ALCOHOL

Ideally, for fast weight loss and for improved health and fitness it is better to avoid alcohol while following the F-Plan.

Realistically, however, if you feel deprived and miserable because you are not allowed any alcohol you will not keep to the diet for long, so it is better to allow yourself a little. Obviously, in terms of calories you can afford to drink more alcohol at one time if you drink only occasionally, at the weekend, perhaps, rather than every day.

Most women can shed weight very successfully on 1,250 calories a day and some can even shed weight on 1,500 calories a day, while nearly all men will achieve a good weight loss on 1,500 calories a day. So most people can allow themselves a little alcohol while they are dieting, should they wish, so long as they set aside 100, 200 or 250 calories for their drinks. This means that a woman who can lose weight successfully on 1,250 or 1,500 calories a day and wants to include an alcoholic drink or two should choose a menu which provides 1,000 or 1,250 calories, thus allowing up to 250 calories for alcoholic drinks. Men should choose a menu of 1,250 to 1,300 calories daily and allow 200 to 250 calories for alcoholic drinks on those days when they know they will want a drink.

On the following pages you will find a calorie chart which will enable you to include drinks as part of your total slimming calorie allowance.

ALCOHOLIC DRINKS CALORIE CHART

	Calories
Aperitifs	
per bar measure (50ml)	
Campari	115
Cinzano bianco	80
Cinzano rosso	75
Dubonnet, red	75
Dubonnet, white	55
Martini, extra dry	55
Martini, sweet	75

	Calories
Aperitifs	
per bottle	
Campari	1,840
Dubonnet, red	1,255
Dubonnet, white	905
Martini, extra dry	905
Martini, sweet	1,255
Beer, Cider and Lager	
per ½ pint (285ml), average value for all types	
Beer, home-brewed	120
Bitter	90
Brown ale	85
Light ale	75
Mild ale	75
Pale ale	90
Cider	100
Lager	90
Lager non-alcoholic (e.g. Barbican)	45
Lager, special brew (e.g. Carlsberg Special Brew)	200
Liqueurs	
per bar measure (25ml)	
Benedictine	90
Cointreau	85
Crème de Menthe	80
Drambuie	85
Grand Marnier	80
Kirsch	50
Tia Maria	75
Port and Sherry	
per small schooner (one third gill, 50ml),	
average value for all types	
Port	75
Sherry, sweet (cream)	65
Sherry, medium	60
Sherry, dry	55
per 75cl bottle	
Port	1,265
Sherry, sweet (cream)	1,100
Sherry, medium	820

	Calories
Port and Sherry	
Sherry, dry	750
Spirits	
per bar measure single	
Whisky, gin, vodka, rum (40° proof)	50
per 75cl bottle	
Whisky, gin, vodka, rum (40° proof)	1,675
Wines	
per 4fl oz (115ml) glass	
Red wine, sweet	95
Red wine, dry	80
Rosé	80
White wine, sweet	100
White wine, dry	75
Champagne	90
per 75cl bottle	
Red wine, sweet	600
Red wine, dry	585
Rosé	585
White wine, sweet	650
White wine, dry	550
Champagne	600

NON-ALCOHOLIC DRINKS CALORIE CHART

	Calories
Beverages	
Fresh milk (whole, pasteurized, sterilized, homogenized, longlife UHT or untreated farm milk), ½ pint (285ml)	180
Fresh milk (semi-skimmed, e.g. Light Gold), ½ pint (285ml)	140
Fresh milk (skimmed), ½ pint (285ml)	90
Dried milk, skimmed, ½ pint (285ml) made up with water	100
Cocoa, 1 rounded teaspoon	20
Drinking chocolate, 1 rounded teaspoon	20
Horlicks, malted milk, 1 rounded teaspoon	20
Ovaltine, 1 heaped teaspoon	25

Calories

Fizzy Drinks and Mixers
All 'low-calorie' labelled drinks (e.g. Energen One Cal
  Drinks, Diet Pepsi, Slimline Tonic) contain negligible
  calories

American Ginger Ale, 4fl oz (115ml)	40
Bitter Lemon, 4fl oz (115ml)	40
Coca Cola	
6¼fl oz (185ml) bottle	80
11½fl oz (325ml) can	140
Dry Ginger Ale, 4fl oz (115ml)	40
Lemonade, ¼ pint (140ml)	50
Pepsi Cola	
6fl oz (170ml) bottle	70
11½fl oz (325ml) can	135
Soda water, per glass	0
Tonic water, 4fl oz (115ml)	40

Fruit Juices
  per 4fl oz (115ml) glass

Apple	40
Grape	60
Grapefruit, bottled, sweetened	65
Grapefruit, canned, sweetened	45
Grapefruit, canned, unsweetened	35
Grapefruit, in a carton, e.g. Just Juice	25
Grapefruit, frozen, reconstituted	45
Orange, bottled, sweetened	70
Orange, canned, sweetened	55
Orange, canned, unsweetened	35
Orange, in a carton, e.g. Just Juice	40
Orange, frozen, reconstituted	60
Pineapple, canned, sweetened	65
Pineapple, bottled, sweetened	65
Tomato, bottled or canned	25

Fruit Squashes and Cordials
  per fl oz (30ml), undiluted

Blackcurrant, cordial	30
Blackcurrant, health drink, e.g. Ribena	85
Lemon barley water	30
Lemon, squash or drink	30
Lime juice, cordial	25
Orange, squash or drink	35
Whole grapefruit drink	30